Words on Being

Sermons 2002-2018

Sarah Sanderson-Doughty

Parson's Porch Books
www.parsonsporchbooks.com

Words on Being: Sermons 2002-2018
ISBN: Softcover 978-1-949888-50-8
Copyright © 2019 by Sarah Sanderson-Doughty

All rights reserved. No part of this book may be reproduced or transmitted in any form or by any means, electronic or mechanical, including photocopying, recording, or by any information storage and retrieval system, without permission in writing from the publisher.

New Revised Standard Version (NRSV), copyright © 1989, The National Council of Churches. Used with permission.

Common English Bible (CEB), copyright © 2011, Christian Resources Development Corporation. Used with permission.

Words on Being

Contents

Introduction 7

Section One-Being God's

Breathe 13
    Genesis 1 (CEB)

If… Then… 17
    Genesis 28:10-22 (NRSV)

God's Giving...21
    Exodus 16:2-15 (NRSV) and Matthew 20:1-16 (NRSV)

You Have a Name...26
    John 20:1-18 (NRSV)

MY Shepherd? 30
    Psalm 23 (NRSV) Mark 6:30-34 (NRSV)

Section Two-Being Human

In or Out?...37
    John 3:1-17 (NSRV); Genesis 12:1-4 (NRSV)

Complicated Hearts 43
    1 Samuel 16:1-13; Psalm 51:10-14

Of This World/Not of This World..48
    John 18:28-40 (CEB)

Being Seen 54
    Luke 7:36-8:3 (NRSV)

Do You Believe This?..58
    John 11:1-45 (NRSV)

Section Three-Being Who God Calls Us to Be

Dancing Prophet 65
    Exodus 3:1-12 (NRSV)

Irresistible Grace 71
    Jonah 3:1-5, 10 (NRSV); Mark 1:14-20 (NRSV)

Company Kept...75
    Luke 15:1-10 (NRSV)

Dealing with Things as They Are 79
    Acts 17:16-31 (CEB)

YES!!!!!! 85
    Psalm 19 (NRSV)

Section Four-Being the Church

Chesed 93
    Ruth 4 (CEB)

It's Not About Me 99
    1 Corinthians 1:10-18 (NRSV)

Fragile Life 104
    1 Corinthians 1:18-25 (NRSV)

Hope for the Church 108
    Ephesians 2:11-21 (NRSV)

Feel and LOVE 113
    Ephesians 4:17-5:2 (CEB)

Section Five-Being Hopeful

Hope 121
    Jeremiah 33:14-16 (NRSV)

No Ifs, Ands or Buts 125
    Luke 24:1-12 (NRSV)

Let Go 128
    John 20:1-18 (NRSV)

Nothing at All 131
    Romans 8:38-39 (NRSV)

Hope in the Resurrection 134
    1 Corinthians 15:12-34 (NRSV)

Index of Sermons by Style 139
Index of Sermons by Seasons 141
Index of Sermons by Churches 142
To Whom They Were Delivered 142
Index of Sermons by Topics/Themes 143

Introduction

The invitation to compile a book of sermons came as a surprise. I have served churches and seminaries now in five states, in five different regions, over the course of sixteen years since my ordination to the ministry of word and sacrament in the Presbyterian Church (USA) in 2002. In every pastoral call I have accepted, I have preached nearly every week, excluding the blessed six Sundays a year gifted for vacation and study leave. Thus, I have quite a well of sermons to which to return for reflection.

When I draw sermons out of the well, I catch glimpses of the people for whom they were written and to whom they were once delivered. I catch glimpses of the moments in time in which they were written. And I catch glimpses of the God who is the source, salvation, and sustenance of all that is.

I also note the variety of preaching styles I have deployed over the years—from more pedagogical and didactic (reflecting my foundational call as a teacher in and for Christ's church) to more dramatic. The diversity in my preaching styles is a mere shadow of the profound diversity that is biblical literature. Preaching always emerges for me out of meditation on and study of specific biblical passages. Different passages yield different sermons, not only different messages, but different ways of carrying the message. Every time I preach, I am seeking to open scripture in such a way that the people I have been called to serve can hear it today. Surely sometimes more successfully than others.

I have tried to gather together in this collection sermons preached to various people, in various places, in various styles, at various times. After distilling my collection of 25 sermons, I realized that many are reflections on being, in one way or another. Hence, I have arranged this book thematically.

First, I offer five sermons on *Being God's*—belonging to God is the more Reformed way to put it! I can't think of a more foundational message than that which is affirmed at the start of the Heidelberg Catechism and the beginning of the Brief Statement of Faith in the PC(USA)— "in life and in death we belong to God." I know this is a theme to which I return repeatedly, and the five sermons gathered in this section are examples off attempts to communicate this foundational message.

In section two, I have gathered five sermons that speak to *Being Human*. These offer different angles on our human condition, both our finitude (limits to knowledge and understanding, as well as our mortality) and our sin (that condition into which we are born, and in which we are entangled, from which only grace can release us).

In section three, the five sermons offered are reflections on *Being Who God Calls Us to Be*. These are all reflections on the grace extended to us in the form of call. As children of God, bound by finitude and entangled in sin, we are all called by God to participate in God's purposes in this world. We can receive calls to specific work, but also to forms of prayer and relationship with God.

In section four, I offer five distinctly ecclesial sermons, all focused on *Being the Church*. If section three focuses on God's call to individuals, section four focuses on God's call to community. I have no greater yearning than for the church to be in our corporate life more fully who we have been baptized to be, for our life together to be a witness to the difference that the life, death, and resurrection of Jesus Christ makes. I know that because we are a human institution, we struggle with finitude and sin and often fall short of God's best purposes for us. The bulk of my preaching, I believe, is focused on helping the church to be the church.

I conclude with a section on *Being Hopeful*. The apostle Paul named love as the greatest gift alongside faith and hope. Surely, love is the greatest gift, but hope is invaluable, utterly precious, and desperately needed. These have not been an easy sixteen years to be in ministry. I began my ministry a year after the horror of 9.11. Wars followed shortly thereafter. Economic inequality has soared. The effects of ecological destruction have been playing out with increasing frequency and intensity. Massive numbers of people have been displaced from their homes and are seeking safe refuge. In recent years the news cycle has been unrelenting and horrifying. National divisions have been deepening and intensifying. And mainline churches have been coming to terms with decades of decline. This is, by no means, an exhaustive litany. But it is a testimony to the challenge of and need for hope. I pray that in some small measure the words on being I offer in the pulpit have helped to give the gift of hope.

None of these sermons, of course, were written for such a thematic arrangement. Many could be shifted to another section quite easily. And other themes can certainly be discerned within them. At the end of the book are several indices to help readers find sermons of styles, written on scriptural material, written for liturgical seasons, written on topics, and written for congregations.

I offer this as a gift to the congregations I have loved, who have faithfully listened throughout the years. I give thanks for the patience of First

Presbyterian Church of Lowville, New York, for enduring with the weekly preaching of a novice preacher – many of the sermons herein were composed for them. I give thanks for the welcome of the First Presbyterian Church of Lebanon, Tennessee for whom I was blessed to preach weekly in a transitional season. I am immensely grateful to the Village Church in Nashville, Tennessee. None of the sermons written originally for this beautiful faith family have found their way to these pages, but members of the Village greatly appreciated the Luke 7 monologue included in section 2 and I am eternally grateful for the welcome to the preaching team and pulpit in this congregation. It was with joy that I preached for the people of First Presbyterian Church of Elkhart, Indiana—both in classic worship in the chapel and sanctuary, and in the emerging service in the Bridge. And it is my immense privilege to be the weekly preacher for St. Andrew's Presbyterian Church in Portland, Oregon now. My father offered me my charge in my first installation service—he quoted the words of his grandmother, my great grandmother Grace— "You've really got to love your people, don't you?" Indeed. And all the words herein were offered and are offered in love.

Section One

Being God's

Breathe
Genesis 1 (CEB)

This sermon was written for and delivered to St. Andrew's Presbyterian Church, in Portland, Oregon, on September 10, 2017, beginning year four of the Narrative lectionary, my preferred lectionary tool in recent years.

Genesis 1 (CEB)

> *1 When God began to create the heavens and the earth—2 the earth was without shape or form, it was dark over the deep sea, and God's wind swept over the waters—3 God said, "Let there be light." And so light appeared. 4 God saw how good the light was. God separated the light from the darkness. 5 God named the light Day and the darkness Night. There was evening and there was morning: the first day. 6 God said, "Let there be a dome in the middle of the waters to separate the waters from each other." 7 God made the dome and separated the waters under the dome from the waters above the dome. And it happened in that way. 8 God named the dome Sky. There was evening and there was morning: the second day. 9 God said, "Let the waters under the sky come together into one place so that the dry land can appear." And that's what happened. 10 God named the dry land Earth, and he named the gathered waters Seas. God saw how good it was. 11 God said, "Let the earth grow plant life: plants yielding seeds and fruit trees bearing fruit with seeds inside it, each according to its kind throughout the earth." And that's what happened. 12 The earth produced plant life: plants yielding seeds, each according to its kind, and trees bearing fruit with seeds inside it, each according to its kind. God saw how good it was. There was evening and there was morning: the third day. 13 God said, "Let there be lights in the dome of the sky to separate the day from the night. They will mark events, sacred seasons, days, and years. 15 They will be lights in the dome of the sky to shine on the earth." And that's what happened.16 God made the stars and two great lights: the larger light to rule over the day and the smaller light to rule over the night. 17 God put them in the dome of the sky to shine on the earth, 18 to rule over the day and over the night, and to separate the light from the darkness. God saw how good it was. 19 There was evening and there was morning: the fourth day.*
>
> *20 God said, "Let the waters swarm with living things, and let birds fly above the earth up in the dome of the sky." 21 God created the great sea animals and all the tiny living things that swarm in the waters,*

each according to its kind, and all the winged birds, each according to its kind. God saw how good it was. 22 Then God blessed them: "Be fertile and multiply and fill the waters in the seas, and let the birds multiply on the earth."

23 There was evening and there was morning: the fifth day.

24 God said, "Let the earth produce every kind of living thing: livestock, crawling things, and wildlife." And that's what happened. 25 God made every kind of wildlife, every kind of livestock, and every kind of creature that crawls on the ground. God saw how good it was. 26 Then God said, "Let us make humanity in our image to resemble us so that they may take charge of the fish of the sea, the birds in the sky, the livestock, all the earth, and all the crawling things on earth."

27 God created humanity in God's own image, in the divine image God created them, male and female God created them. 28 God blessed them and said to them, "Be fertile and multiply; fill the earth and master it. Take charge of the fish of the sea, the birds in the sky, and everything crawling on the ground." 29 Then God said, "I now give to you all the plants on the earth that yield seeds and all the trees whose fruit produces its seeds within it. These will be your food. 30 To all wildlife, to all the birds in the sky, and to everything crawling on the ground—to everything that breathes—I give all the green grasses for food." And that's what happened. 31 God saw everything he had made: it was supremely good.

There was evening and there was morning: the sixth day.

***

It's been hard to breathe this week—quite literally as thick smoke has filled our air as the beloved gorge has been on fire, a fire triggered by the carelessness of a youngster. But it's been hard to breathe spiritually as well— as we process news of the flooding in Texas and anticipate the ravages of Hurricane Irma, a storm the size of the state of Ohio in the Caribbean and possibly in Florida as well, as we tremble with news of North Korea's sixth nuclear test and the awareness that they have the capacity to strike our own nation, as battles rage over immigration and decisions leave young people's lives hanging in the balance. It's been hard to breathe, deeply, for a while now, with the awareness of hateful, white supremacist ideology emboldened in our nation and conflict erupting on our nations' streets. And perhaps it has been hard to breathe in St. A's as you have endured so many losses this past year, saying yet another goodbye just last week.

So, focusing on the poetry of Genesis 1 and the beginning of Genesis 2 might feel a bit dissonant today. Our Bibles begin with a poetic celebration of God as the source of all that is… and a poetic affirmation of the goodness of God's creation, all of God's creation—living and non-living—every creature, every dimension of creation, every human being created in the image of God… Through this poetry we affirm that this world, this universe, it all belongs to God. And it is all beloved of God.

We look around right now, gasping for breath, and it might be hard to throw ourselves into this affirmation. But here's something I learned anew this week—this poem wasn't written at the beginning of all that is… nothing was, of course. It wasn't even written at the beginning of the history of the people of Israel… it was written during the *exile* of the people of Israel—when their kingdom had crumbled, their temple had been destroyed, their leaders dispersed to foreign lands… It was written at a time when it may have been hard for Israel to catch their breath—the ruach—the Spirit of God.

And yet the Spirit flowed through them into the poem with which our Bible begins… I appreciated this interpretation of the beginning of Genesis offered by the curriculum we are using for worship planning and children's ministry, I quote, "It is not ever meant to be an explanation of creation but an answer to a question asking the faithful remnant: do you still believe your God is powerful enough to protect you? When in exile you can let God go or let God grow, rethinking who God is in a strange and foreign land. This poem, written when they had to rethink what they believed about God now that God's indestructible house, Jerusalem and the temple, had been destroyed. This poem is a loud shout and faithful response to that question with the answer: 'Yes! We do!'"

So, it is good for us to return to the beginning because this too is a moment when we, a faithful remnant, are asked 'Do you still believe your God is powerful enough to protect you?" It is a moment for letting God grow, for affirming that this world, this universe, and everybody and everything in it is God's good creation, in God's hands. If Israel could do it in exile, we can do it today.

So, we launch Children's Ministry anew, and sign up to volunteer to serve our neighbors, and engage in fellowship in our courtyard. So, the choir resumes its singing and strategic planning with hope for the future begins. And so, three people are beginning anew their walk with God by committing themselves to membership in this congregation. We begin anew today—all of us—because we believe in God our creator, revealed in Jesus our Savior, experienced by the breath of God that moves through us—the Holy Spirit. Take a moment to breathe right now. Deeply. Again. Again. Again.

Know that this world belongs to God.

Know that this church belongs to God.

Know that you belong to God.

Breathe.

Resource in addition to scripture that was cited in this sermon

The curriculum quoted is *Spill the Beans: Worship and Learning Resources for All Ages*, a resource prepared by people in the church of Scotland and accessible through http://spillbeans.org.uk/ The quote in this sermon can be found in the Bible Notes on pg. 6 in Issue 24.

If... Then...
Genesis 28:10-22 (NRSV)

This sermon was originally written for the First Presbyterian Church of Lowville, New York and delivered during a stewardship campaign on October 16, 2005. I have delivered it in other churches as well. It is one of my more dramatic sermons and I typically memorize it for delivery.

> *10 Jacob left Beer-Sheba and went toward Haran. 11 He came to a certain place and stayed there for the night, because the sun had set. Taking one of the stones of the place, he put it under his head and lay down in that place. 12 And he dreamed that there was a ladder set up on the earth, the top of it reaching to heaven; and the angels of God were ascending and descending on it. 13 And the Lord stood beside him and said, "I am the Lord, the God of Abraham your father and the God of Isaac; the land on which you lie I will give to you and to your offspring; 14 and your offspring shall be like the dust of the earth, and you shall spread abroad to the west and to the east and to the north and to the south; and all the families of the earth shall be blessed in you and in your offspring. 15 Know that I am with you and will keep you wherever you go, and will bring you back to this land; for I will not leave you until I have done what I have promised you." 16 Then Jacob woke from his sleep and said, "Surely the Lord is in this place—and I did not know it!" 17 And he was afraid, and said, "How awesome is this place! This is none other than the house of God, and this is the gate of heaven."*
>
> *18 So Jacob rose early in the morning, and he took the stone that he had put under his head and set it up for a pillar and poured oil on the top of it. 19 He called that place Bethel; but the name of the city was Luz at the first. 20 Then Jacob made a vow, saying, "If God will be with me, and will keep me in this way that I go, and will give me bread to eat and clothing to wear, 21 so that I come again to my father's house in peace, then the Lord shall be my God, 22 and this stone, which I have set up for a pillar, shall be God's house; and of all that you give me I will surely give one-tenth to you."*

***

You're on a journey, all alone. The sun goes down. You grab a stone for a pillow and lie down to sleep. And wham, bam, in one night's sleep your whole world changes. Just yesterday you were engaged in an intricate plot to deceive your father into giving you the blessing that rightly belonged to your brother. Just yesterday you lied to your blind father, disguising yourself, suggesting to him that the meat that you offered him to eat you had caught yourself and killed and prepared for him, when really your mother took care of it all. When your father wondered how you could have succeeded in your hunt so quickly, you chose these words for your lie 'Because the Lord YOUR God granted me success". Just yesterday your brother brought his offering to your father too late, the dawning awareness of deception brought rage to their hearts. Just yesterday your mother devised a means to get you out of town so to protect you from your hurting brother, she sent you to find a wife from among your grandfather's descendants. She sent you alone on a long journey, fleeing for a wife, fleeing for your life. You had no intention of taking this journey. You had no choice. And the sun went down; you had to stop; you took a stone; you slept; you dreamt. And everything changed.

You came into this world grabbing, grabbing your brother's heel, you continued to grab. You heard tell of promises... blessings... as you grew... you grabbed after them, not realizing promises and blessings can't be grabbed, ripped by one human hand from another. Not realizing the source of the promises and blessings you sought. Not realizing this God your father talked about was for real. You grabbed. You cheated. You lied. Because you were sure it was each man for himself in this world and your brother was your first competitor.

For a moment there it had seemed like you had won, like you had finally grabbed something worth grabbing, but now here you are all alone in a strange city, with your head on a rock, sleeping under the stars. And as you laid down your head, you thought of your brother safe at home with his three wives and with your mom and dad you began to wonder just what your grabbing had gotten you... a heart racing with fear, a lonely night, words from a father, a stone for a pillow, a whole lot of nothing. You dampened that stone with your tears as you fell asleep, sure that you were alone in this world.

But then the dream. You can see that ladder reaching to heaven. You can see the angels climbing up and down it, you wonder who else might come down that great big ladder. Your head is tilted back looking up, up, up. Your mouth is open. You nearly jump when you hear the voice coming from beside you. You dare not look when the stranger gives a name. "I am the LORD, the God of Abraham your father and the God of Isaac; the land on which you lie I will give to you and to your offspring; and your offspring shall be like the dust of the earth, and you shall spread abroad to the west and to the east, to the north and to the south; and all the families of the earth shall be blessed in you and your offspring. Know that I am with you and will keep you wherever you go and will bring you back to this land for I will not leave you until I have done what I promised you."

The power of these words shakes you from sleep. There it was. What you had been grabbing after your whole life, promise, blessing... and yet you had ceased your grabbing, you surrendered to tears and to sleep... and now... now it happens? 'Surely the LORD is in this place and I did not know it." You tremble. You shake. The awe, the fear is overwhelming. 'Perhaps the LORD has always been with me and I did not know it," you think, but dare not speak. 'How awesome is this place! This is none other than the house of God and the gate of heaven," you declare through your fear and trembling.

You arise early in the morning. You take that stone, your tears now dried upon it. You set it up as a pillar and dampen it again now not with tears, but with oil. The pillow becomes a pillar, a memorial, a lasting marker of the presence of God in this place. This is not enough. You must do more to mark this place as holy. So, you change its name to Bethel-house of God. Those residing in the city still call it Luz, almond tree-but you know better. You know that this is where God dwells.

You stand back and admire your pillar. And then you think about what God said to you. 'Know that I am with you and will keep you wherever you go and will bring you back to this land for I will not leave you until I have done what I promised you." God doesn't just dwell here, in this place. God dwells with you, in you, and God will always be with you.

You fall to your knees as the weight of this promise sinks in. You will never be alone. You will be cared for wherever you go. You will have bread to eat and clothes to wear. You will, someday, be able to do what seemed impossible just yesterday, you will be able to return to your father's house in peace, you will reconcile with your family. This is what this means. The words tumble out of your mouth as the new day dawns 'If God will be with me, and will keep me in this way that I go, and will give me bread to eat and clothing to wear, so that I come again to my father's house in peace, THEN the LORD shall be MY God, and this stone which I have set up for a pillar shall be God's house; and of all that you give me I shall surely give one tenth to you." Just yesterday this God was your father's God, but now this God is your God. You can't help but worship. You can't help but create a home for worship. You can't help but give at least 10% of all that God has given you back. It just makes sense. God doesn't demand this promise of you. God doesn't grab. God gives and when you realize ALL that God gives, you can't help but give too. What's 10%? Just the beginning of gratitude.

God IS with you. God DOES keep you in the way that you go. God DOES feed and clothe you. GOD WILL BE WITH YOU UNTIL ALL THAT GOD HAS PROMISED YOU IS FULFILLED! GOD, THE CREATOR, REDEEMER, AND SUSTAINER OF THE UNIVERSE IS WITH YOU! How can you not worship, how can you not build a home for God, how can you not give back to God one tenth of all that God has given you? In Jesus' name.

God's Giving
Exodus 16:2-15 (NRSV) and Matthew 20:1-16 (NRSV)

This sermon was written for and delivered to the First Presbyterian Church of Lowville, NY on September 18, 2005.

Exodus 16:2-15

> *2 The whole congregation of the Israelites complained against Moses and Aaron in the wilderness. 3 The Israelites said to them, "If only we had died by the hand of the Lord in the land of Egypt, when we sat by the fleshpots and ate our fill of bread; for you have brought us out into this wilderness to kill this whole assembly with hunger."*
>
> *4 Then the Lord said to Moses, "I am going to rain bread from heaven for you, and each day the people shall go out and gather enough for that day. In that way I will test them, whether they will follow my instruction or not. 5 On the sixth day, when they prepare what they bring in, it will be twice as much as they gather on other days." 6 So Moses and Aaron said to all the Israelites, "In the evening you shall know that it was the Lord who brought you out of the land of Egypt, 7 and in the morning you shall see the glory of the Lord, because he has heard your complaining against the Lord. For what are we, that you complain against us?" 8 And Moses said, "When the Lord gives you meat to eat in the evening and your fill of bread in the morning, because the Lord has heard the complaining that you utter against him—what are we? Your complaining is not against us but against the Lord."*
>
> *9 Then Moses said to Aaron, "Say to the whole congregation of the Israelites, 'Draw near to the Lord, for he has heard your complaining.'" 10 And as Aaron spoke to the whole congregation of the Israelites, they looked toward the wilderness, and the glory of the Lord appeared in the cloud. 11 The Lord spoke to Moses and said, 12 "I have heard the complaining of the Israelites; say to them, 'At twilight you shall eat meat, and in the morning you shall have your fill of bread; then you shall know that I am the Lord your God.'"*
>
> *13 In the evening quails came up and covered the camp; and in the morning there was a layer of dew around the camp. 14 When the layer of dew lifted, there on the surface of the wilderness was a fine flaky substance, as fine as frost on the ground. 15 When the Israelites saw it, they said to one another, "What is it?" For they did not know what*

it was. Moses said to them, "It is the bread that the Lord has given you to eat.

Matthew 20:1-16 (NRSV)

20 "For the kingdom of heaven is like a landowner who went out early in the morning to hire laborers for his vineyard. 2 After agreeing with the laborers for the usual daily wage, he sent them into his vineyard. 3 When he went out about nine o'clock, he saw others standing idle in the marketplace; 4 and he said to them, 'You also go into the vineyard, and I will pay you whatever is right.' So, they went. 5 When he went out again about noon and about three o'clock, he did the same. 6 And about five o'clock he went out and found others standing around; and he said to them, 'Why are you standing here idle all day?' 7 They said to him, 'Because no one has hired us.' He said to them, 'You also go into the vineyard.' 8 When evening came, the owner of the vineyard said to his manager, 'Call the laborers and give them their pay, beginning with the last and then going to the first.' 9 When those hired about five o'clock came, each of them received the usual daily wage. 10 Now when the first came, they thought they would receive more; but each of them also received the usual daily wage. 11 And when they received it, they grumbled against the landowner, 12 saying, 'These last worked only one hour, and you have made them equal to us who have borne the burden of the day and the scorching heat.' 13 But he replied to one of them, 'Friend, I am doing you no wrong; did you not agree with me for the usual daily wage? 14 Take what belongs to you and go; I choose to give to this last the same as I give to you. 15 Am I not allowed to do what I choose with what belongs to me? Or are you envious because I am generous?' 16 So the last will be first, and the first will be last."

***

A month ago, they were dancing on the shores of the sea that had miraculously opened and closed, closing the deal on their promised freedom. The hooting and hollering that day by the sea was raucous; many wept crocodile tears of joy, and gleeful songs rang out-no more brick making, no more heavy labor forced upon them by the Egyptians, no more slavery. There is a God, a God of love, a God of salvation, Alleluia!

But now thirty days have come and gone and the joy that led to dancing by the sea somehow drained away as the trek -to where? -unfolded. The conditions were dreadful. A whole month in the wilderness -the dry, cracked, bitter, forbidding wilderness. The unleavened bread packed in haste disappeared all too quickly. By now the children are weeping and the adults are grumbling giving voice to their empty stomachs, their sore feet, their exhaustion. The complaint revolts against Moses and Aaron, their God given leaders, "It would have been better to die in Egypt where at least we had food to eat, but no... you had to bring us out here into this bitter wilderness to kill us all with hunger." Moses and Aaron were hungry too.

They complained to Moses and Aaron, but God was listening. "Ahem-Moses. I have this under control. You'll be receiving a regular shipment of bread from heaven, enough for all the people to get just what they need for the day, every day -not more, not less. On the eve of the sabbath they should collect double to carry them through the day of rest. Keep their eyes on me. Over and out."

So, Moses takes this message to the people. "People it's God who brought us out of slavery, it's God who will keep us alive. You will know this in the morning. You will know this in the night. Don't look to us, your leaders, we are but servants of God. Look to God. God will give you meat in the evening and bread in the morning. God has heard your complaint. Your complaint is not with us. It is with God." Aaron then speaks for Moses "Draw near to the Lord for he has heard your complaining."

They try to draw near to God, but they are weary, and they don't really know how. They look vaguely toward the wilderness and there they see that God has drawn near to them, they see the glory of God in a cloud. And by night quails filled the camp, more than enough to ensure they would all eat and by morning bread fell from heaven, bread like nothing they had ever seen before, enough to fill their bellies. God gives enough for all to live.

***

There's work to be done, a harvest to be brought in. Many laborers are needed. The landowner himself, not his manager, not a hired hand, but the landowner himself goes out to find some workers. He's out before the crack of dawn and so are many eager workers. He gathers several together and sends into the vineyard with a promise of a day's wage - enough to live on - nothing more, nothing less.

A few hours pass and though these early workers are working hard there is so much more work to be done. The landowner goes back to the marketplace where workers gather and calls forth some who were standing idle there "I have work that needs to be done and you need work to do. Go into the vineyard, I'll pay you whatever is right." They go.

The landowner takes stock of progress midday and sees he still has need for more workers - the harvest is plentiful; the laborers are few. So back to the marketplace he goes where he finds more who are idle and sets them to work. Three hours later he does the same. And at five o'clock, 11 hours after the work day began, an hour before it was to close, there was still more work to be done, still more workers without work, workers who had waited all day and no one had been willing to hire them, and so the landowner sends even these into the vineyard.

When the sun begins to set, it is time to pay the workers their wages. It is time for the workers to return home to feed their families which their daily pay will hopefully make possible. The landowner tells his manager 'Call the laborers and give them their pay, beginning with the last and then going to the first." Those hired later in the day have no idea what they will be paid, the landowner simply said he will pay them what is right. Each worker is paid the same, one denarius, a fair day's wage, just enough to live on, whether they worked an hour or twelve, their basic needs are met. Surely those who worked only an hour walk away with a spring in their step. When they had sweat in the marketplace as the hours rolled by, they had been sure there would be nothing to feed their families that night, but now they are going home to fill some bellies. But those who had worked since six a.m. had a bone to pick with the landowner. Sure, they had only been promised to be paid a day's wage, promised to be paid what they need to live on, but 'this is not fair! Our twelve hours to their one earns the same pay???!"

But let's not lose sight of the landowner, he gave them all meaningful work that day, he paid them all what is required for basic sustenance, he gave them enough to fill the bellies of their families, he gave them all enough to live.

***

It's 2005 and this congregation has been on a journey together for nearly 200 years. There have been moments in this rich history when all assembled were able to say 'Glory be! Praise the Lord! God is good. God provides." Yes, there have surely been moments when such affirmations have rolled from the tongues of those who filled these pews. But there have also been moments when some have extolled the glories of God while others have grumbled, moments when the distribution of God's blessings was deemed unfair or inappropriate. And there have also been moments when everybody was grumbling, blaming the pastor, the elders for leading them into a wilderness where they could not feel or trust in God's presence and providence.

It is tempting, in our life together as the people of God, to look to one another to assess the state of God's blessings. If our neighbor is grumbling or has stopped attending church or is organizing a protest, then surely God has withdrawn God's blessing. If our neighbor is smiling, singing with glee, signing up to feed the hungry then surely God is showering God's blessings upon us. If one neighbor is grumbling and one neighbor is praising Jesus, then we don't know what to think and can grow anxious and confused.

Here's the thing: we're always called to look to God, not just when we're conscious of the blessings flowing down, but all the time. We're called to look to God and consider God's giving. Did you survive yesterday? How did you do that? You may have put in an hour of exercise, brushed your teeth, paid your taxes, and mowed the lawn, but that's not what made it possible for you to survive. You may have shown love to your spouse or your kids or your neighbors or a stranger, but that's not what made it possible for you to survive. You may have eaten three square meals, or maybe only one, or maybe just the free cheesecake at the cream cheese festival, but even that is not what made it possible for you to survive. Yesterday and the day before that and the day before that and the day before that you were given just what you needed to live by God.

That's how God gives. God gives life.

Sometimes we may experience this in abundance. Sometimes we may feel we're getting just enough to scrape by. But every morning we wake up still drawing breath, every evening we go to bed heart still beating, we are recipients of God's giving and grace. When we look to God and to God's giving, we are always and forever grateful. When we take our eyes off God and get distracted by apparent inequities, injustices, unfairness all sorts of other feelings creep in anxiety, insecurity, jealousy, bitterness, resentment, rage, all of which are acid that eat away at gratitude and harden our hearts.

There is enough for all of us and that is why we are all here today, lungs expanding and contracting, hearts beating, minds seeking. If we have complaints, let us lift them to God. If we have praises, let us lift them to God. Let us draw near to God, for God has drawn near to us. In Jesus' name. Amen.

You Have a Name
John 20:1-18 (NRSV)

This sermon was originally written for and delivered to the First Presbyterian Church of Lowville, New York on Easter Sunday 2006.

John 20:1-18 (NRSV)

20 Early on the first day of the week, while it was still dark, Mary Magdalene came to the tomb and saw that the stone had been removed from the tomb. 2 So she ran and went to Simon Peter and the other disciple, the one whom Jesus loved, and said to them, "They have taken the Lord out of the tomb, and we do not know where they have laid him." 3 Then Peter and the other disciple set out and went toward the tomb. 4 The two were running together, but the other disciple outran Peter and reached the tomb first. 5 He bent down to look in and saw the linen wrappings lying there, but he did not go in. 6 Then Simon Peter came, following him, and went into the tomb. He saw the linen wrappings lying there, 7 and the cloth that had been on Jesus' head, not lying with the linen wrappings but rolled up in a place by itself. 8 Then the other disciple, who reached the tomb first, also went in, and he saw and believed; 9 for yet they did not understand the scripture, that he must rise from the dead. 10 Then the disciples returned to their homes.

11 But Mary stood weeping outside the tomb. As she wept, she bent over to investigate the tomb; 12 and she saw two angels in white, sitting where the body of Jesus had been lying, one at the head and the other at the feet. 13 They said to her, "Woman, why are you weeping?" She said to them, "They have taken away my Lord, and I do not know where they have laid him." 14 When she had said this, she turned around and saw Jesus standing there, but she did not know that it was Jesus. 15 Jesus said to her, "Woman, why are you weeping? Whom are you looking for?" Supposing him to be the gardener, she said to him, "Sir, if you have carried him away, tell me where you have laid him, and I will take him away." 16 Jesus said to her, "Mary!" She turned and said to him in Hebrew, "Rabbouni!" (which means Teacher). 17 Jesus said to her, "Do not hold on to me, because I have not yet ascended to the Father. But go to my brothers and say to them, 'I am ascending to my Father and your Father, to my God and your God.'" 18 Mary Magdalene went and announced to the disciples, "I have seen the Lord"; and she told them that he had said these things to her.

***

"I know you, but you don't have a name" the spry and spunky 103-year-old declared when she saw her niece-in-law at the grocery store. This brought laughter to the niece and laughter to those with whom the niece shared the story. At 103, we figure, one is entitled for forget a name now and again. My dear Kevin would say at 33 one is entitled to forget a name now and again.

But consider the power of knowing a name, the difference it makes when someone smiles broadly, stretches out a hand and calls you by name, the difference it makes when you want to offer comfort and you're able to say 'I'm praying for you, Sam" as you reach out and gently pat a back. When someone knows our names, we feel cherished, valued, honored... when someone messes up our names or forgets them completely, we can feel devalued or dishonored.

Sometimes a name is all that is needed for recognition to be achieved after time or distance has separated one from another. A few weeks ago, I was at a concert in Syracuse with Kevin and a friend whom I have not seen for over a decade was also there. I had heard she would be there, so I knew to look for her, but I don't think she had any preparation. I walked up to her. I smiled. She smiled. But in her eyes, I could see confusion, the creases around her eyes said, "I know you, but you don't have a name." I said 'Sarah Sanderson" and she relaxed and said "Oh, of course...." we embraced and reconnected. The name was the key that opened the door.

Mary was a mess that morning at the tomb. She hadn't slept in days. She was just beginning to accept the fact that her beloved teacher Jesus was truly dead when she made her way to the tomb before sunrise. She had certain expectations. She expected that she would find a heavy stone rolled across the mouth of the cave. She expected that should she find someone to roll the stone away that she would see the body of her beloved teacher, wounded, decaying, lying there dead. She expected that this visit to the tomb would invite another round of tears, her eyes still swollen, her chest still aching from all the crying she'd already done. So, when through the darkness she could make out that the stone had been rolled away, she was immediately distressed. Her first expectation crushed under the weight of that heavy stone that had been rolled away. She ran away as fast as she could. She didn't look inside the tomb to see if he was there, she automatically assumed that if her first expectation was crushed then her second expectation would be crushed as well. "They have taken our Lord away and I don't know where they have laid him." Two of the men run back to the tomb with her. They investigate and find that in fact his body is gone, the linens in which it had been wrapped lying empty there. They return to their hiding places. Mary is frozen there weeping, the only expectation that managed to be fulfilled. She looks inside the tomb. It can't be. He must be in there. And two angels greet her. "Woman, why are you weeping?" "They have taken away my Lord and I don't know where they have laid him." She turns around as if continuing her search and whom she seeks is right in front of her, but she cannot see him, she cannot recognize him, until.... he calls her by name, "Mary". Her name is the key that opens the door to recognition, that allows embrace and reconnection. With this simple act Jesus says to Mary "I know you, and you have a name."

Mary struggled to recognize the risen Christ even when he was standing right in front of her. We have our own struggles recognizing the risen Christ. Jane Thomas shared a story at one of the women's holy week services this year about a young mission volunteer in the Philippines who had become rather numb to the whole idea of resurrection. After hearing about it every week her entire life, it ceased to be especially good news becoming, rather, old news. For some the struggle of Easter is the struggle of this young woman; we are jaded, numb to the shocking revelation of resurrection. For some though, the struggle is to believe, it just sounds too ridiculous, too farfetched, too, too... impossible. Whether we have heard the story so often that it cannot grab us because our expectations get in the way or whether the story is so new to us that it cannot grab us because other earthly expectations get in the way, whatever the case may be, it can be difficult for those who find themselves in pews in Presbyterian churches in the United States of America in the 21st century to feel connected, embraced.

I believe that the only way we'll truly be moved to shout and sing alleluias on this Easter morn, whether we're hearing the story for the zillionth time or the first, is if we know that the living Christ is right here for each of us, saying "I know you and you have a name."

Frederick Buechner tells the story of going to receive communion at a church where his friend was the priest. He was kneeling at the rail and could hear the priest saying "The body of Christ for you. The blood of Christ for you." repeatedly. But then he heard the strangest thing, right in front of him, "The body of Christ for you Freddy. The blood of Christ for you." He was totally shaken by this, not only that he was called by name, but that he was called by the most personal, intimate name anyone ever called him. He wasn't just an anonymous so and so at the rail. He was a person, a real person who made mistakes and who did some beautiful things, a real person, with a name. In that moment it became clear that Jesus KNOWS him, knows him as he really is, and is for him. All this was communicated in a name.

Each person here is precious and beloved in God's sight. God knows you and you have names. The risen Christ greets not only Mary, but each of us, by name, not only today, but every day. You received a nametag with your bulletin today. If you haven't done so already, please fill it out and stick it on your Easter finest. You don't have to write your formal name on the tag, write the name that suits you best, maybe it's a nickname, maybe it's a middle name, write the name that unlocks the door to your heart. And if you don't write your name, be prepared to be asked for your name when you come forward for communion because the bread of life and the cup of salvation, Jesus Christ with us in bread and cup is for you, and you have a name.

MY Shepherd?
Psalm 23 (NRSV) Mark 6:30-34 (NRSV)

This sermon was written for and delivered to the First Presbyterian Church of Lowville, NY on Sunday, July 23, 2006. I distinctly remember the study for this sermon on our front porch swing.

Mark 6:30-34

> *30 The apostles gathered around Jesus and told him all that they had done and taught. 31 He said to them, "Come away to a deserted place all by yourselves and rest a while." For many were coming and going, and they had no leisure even to eat. 32 And they went away in the boat to a deserted place by themselves. 33 Now many saw them going and recognized them, and they hurried there on foot from all the towns and arrived ahead of them. 34 As he went ashore, he saw a great crowd; and he had compassion for them, because they were like sheep without a shepherd; and he began to teach them many things.*

Psalm 23

> *1 The Lord is my shepherd, I shall not want. 2 He makes me lie down in green pastures he leads me beside still waters; 3 he restores my soul. He leads me in right paths for his name's sake. 4 Even though I walk through the darkest valley, 5 I fear no evil for you are with me; your rod and your staff—they comfort me. 6 You prepare a table before me in the presence of my enemies; you anoint my head with oil; my cup overflows. 7 Surely goodness and mercy shall follow me all the days of my life and I shall dwell in the house of the Lord my whole life long.*

***

On some mornings when I don't have to get an early start, I like to lie in bed and awaken slowly to the morning news on the radio. Usually I only end up catching bits and pieces, fragments here and there, but eventually a story catches my interest and draws me up from the depths of drowsiness to pay attention. On Wednesday morning this week, three stories in a row grabbed me and shook me awake. First, I heard of children in Lebanon who were simultaneously scared and excited by the bombs falling all around them; then I heard the death count in this Israeli-Lebanese conflict was already over 400, the conflict threatening to spill over the rim of Lebanon. Then I heard of the rapidly escalating civilian death count in Iraq; I heard of a bomb made from a teenage girl's head. And then, a little closer to home, I heard of patients that were murdered by their caregivers in a New Orleans hospital in the aftermath of Katrina. I don't feel fear all the time, but I felt it that morning. I felt it in my bones. I needed comfort, solace, peace.

For generations Christians who have needed comfort, solace, peace have found a taste of what they were seeking in the 23rd Psalm. It's remarkable the way the spirit in the air changes when these words are read bedside, graveside, or when one is all alone and shaking with fear. "The Lord is MY shepherd. I shall not want. He makes me lie down in green pastures. He leads me beside still waters. He restores my soul. Even though I walk through the valley of darkness I will fear no evil for You are with me, your rod and your staff they comfort me. You prepare a table before me in the presence of my enemies. You anoint my head with oil. My cup overflows. Surely goodness and mercy shall follow me all the days of my life and I shall live in the house of the Lord my whole life long." He is MY shepherd. He leads ME. He restores ME. He comforts ME. He feeds ME. He anoints ME. The spirit in the air always lightens. Hope returns. It's remarkable the power of this Psalm.

Surely if it has had this effect for so many generations of Christians, is it so hard to imagine that it might have had that effect on generations of Jews prior even to the coming of Christ. I spent some time this week trying to put myself in the shoes of the apostles in today's Gospel passage. They've just come back to Jesus after who knows how many days of looking people in the eyes and telling them they need to turn their lives around, after who knows how many demons have flown in their faces, after who knows how much sickness they have confronted and healed. They've come back to Jesus after word about their ministry had found its way to murderous King Herod, the one who not too long before had ordered the serving up of John the Baptist's head on a platter. They had to be exhausted and afraid. I can see them muttering the words of the 23rd Psalm as they made their way back to Jesus "The Lord is my shepherd... Even though I walk through the valley of darkness... "And I can see the relief in their faces when Jesus looks at them, listens to them and says, 'Come away to a deserted place all by yourselves and rest awhile.'" They aren't certain, but they have a sense, deep down, that maybe they've found their shepherd. They have this sense as he leads them across the waters, so they can find rest for their souls, and perhaps some food for their grumbling bellies as well.

That spirit change must have been taking place in that boat but imagine how quickly it changed back when they caught sight of the shore of their supposedly deserted place and saw it swarming with people. I can feel their frustration. "But Jesus you said we were going to get away from it all for a while. Where did all these people come from? We can't take it anymore. It's too intense. We're too exhausted. We're so afraid." But Jesus is looking at all those people on the shore just as he looked at his twelve apostles not too long before, he is looking at them with compassion, these people he sees are like sheep without a shepherd. So, he wastes not a moment. He sets to teaching them. I can see the apostles sitting sullen as Jesus teaches. Still hungry. Still needing rest. And they are none too happy about having to wait any longer for their needs to be met. So as soon as the sun starts to set, they see their opportunity.

"Hey Jesus, it's getting late, why don't you send these people off to get something to eat?"

Imagine their irritation when Jesus says, "You give them something to eat." "Who us? What are we supposed to do-go drop a ridiculous amount of money on bread to feed all of THEM? Are you crazy? And what about US, Jesus? I thought the point was for US to be fed and get rest." "How much bread do you have? Go and see." They take stock and briefly think they may be off the hook 'Five loaves and two fish, just about enough for US Jesus, and barely that." But then Jesus does the strangest thing, he has them organize the crowd into groups of fifties and hundreds, there were about 5,000 in all, maybe more. He has them seat the groups down on the soft green grass. And then he blesses and breaks the bread as if he were at a dinner table with all these guests and has the apostles pass it around. They think he's crazy, but somehow EVERYONE there is fed, and when they all are satisfied the apostles gather up leftovers and all in all there are twelve baskets full of broken bread and fish. Twelve baskets for twelve apostles who can now lie down on the soft green grass and eat their fill.

All get to lie down in green pastures, by still waters, all have their souls restored, all are comforted, a table is set for all even as the evil hangs in the air, all are shepherded. The apostles felt themselves in need of a shepherd, but they had a shepherd, those in that gigantic crowd did not and Jesus needed the help of the 12 to shepherd all in that crowd, the 12 did not lose their shepherd, they simply helped 5,000 gain one.

So, while I may be tempted, considering the week's news, to curl up into a ball and repeat the words of the 23rd Psalm repeatedly seeking the peace that only my Shepherd can give. While you might be tempted to focus on finding green pastures and still waters for the restoration of your soul. While we might be tempted to have a feast here with familiar faces, even as evil hangs all around us. It doesn't quite work that way. There's a massive crowd in this world who are like sheep without a shepherd and our shepherd looks on them with compassion and asks us to help the shepherding along. We who have a shepherd, who trust in green pastures, and still waters, and heavenly feasts, we are asked to share these precious gifts with those who need them. Jesus provides them. Jesus is the shepherd. We simply need share them.

Because the Lord is not just MY Shepherd. The Lord is the shepherd for ALL the sheep without one. The Lord is not just YOUR shepherd. The Lord is the shepherd for ALL the sheep who need one. The Lord is not just OUR shepherd. The Lord is the shepherd for ALL who are lost, afraid, surrounded by enemies, and in need of a meal. NONE shall want. ALL shall be made to lie down in green pastures, ALL shall be led beside still waters, ALL shall have their souls restored, God is with ALL, ALL shall be comforted, ALL shall feast.

Section Two

Being Human

In or Out?
John 3:1-17 (NSRV); Genesis 12:1-4 (NRSV)

I originally wrote this sermon for the McCormick Seminary community in 2002, my senior year. I was delighted to revisit it when I candidated for the pastoral opening at St. Andrew's Presbyterian Church on the first Sunday in Lent in 2017. This is the revised sermon I used for that occasion.

John 3:1-17 (NRSV)

3 Now there was a Pharisee named Nicodemus, a leader of the Jews. 2 He came to Jesus by night and said to him, "Rabbi, we know that you are a teacher who has come from God; for no one can do these signs that you do apart from the presence of God." 3 Jesus answered him, "Very truly, I tell you, no one can see the kingdom of God without being born from above." 4 Nicodemus said to him, "How can anyone be born after having grown old? Can one enter a second time into the mother's womb and be born?" 5 Jesus answered, "Very truly, I tell you, no one can enter the kingdom of God without being born of water and Spirit. 6 What is born of the flesh is flesh, and what is born of the Spirit is spirit. 7 Do not be astonished that I said to you, 'You must be born from above.' 8 The wind blows where it chooses, and you hear the sound of it, but you do not know where it comes from or where it goes. So, it is with everyone who is born of the Spirit." 9 Nicodemus said to him, "How can these things be?" 10 Jesus answered him, "Are you a teacher of Israel, and yet you do not understand these things?

11 "Very truly, I tell you, we speak of what we know and testify to what we have seen; yet you do not receive our testimony. 12 If I have told you about earthly things and you do not believe; how can you believe if I tell you about heavenly things? 13 No one has ascended into heaven except the one who descended from heaven, the Son of Man. 14 And just as Moses lifted the serpent in the wilderness, so must the Son of Man be lifted, 15 that whoever believes in him may have eternal life.

16 "For God so loved the world that he gave his only Son, so that everyone who believes in him may not perish but may have eternal life. 17 "Indeed, God did not send the Son into the world to condemn the world, but in order that the world might be saved through him.

Genesis 12:1-4 (NRSV)

12 Now the Lord said to Abram, "Go from your country and your kindred and your father's house to the land that I will show you. 2 I will make of you a great nation, and I will bless you, and make your name great, so that you will be a blessing. 3 I will bless those who bless you, and the one who curses you I will curse; and in you all the families of the earth shall be blessed."

4 So Abram went, as the Lord had told him; and Lot went with him. Abram was seventy-five years old when he departed from Haran.

***

We have recently entered the season of Lent and for our Lenten reflection, for our journeys in faith, God offers us these words from Genesis and John. Thanks to an atonement class I took in seminary, I can no longer approach this season without seriously contemplating what it is that God has done in Jesus Christ. I can no longer read scripture in these holy weeks without wondering what it reveals about the meaning of the cross and the empty tomb. We call Christ, Savior, and have long understood the cross and empty tomb to be symbols of salvation, but what does that mean to us today? What is salvation? What is the nature of Christ's saving work? And the question that this week's scripture raises is—who is saved and who is not? Who is in and who is out?

Now this is not a question about which progressive Christians spend much time thinking. We get a bit creeped out by people who talk about being saved, and ask strangers, or even people of other professed religious belief if they are saved. We're more likely to talk about liberation than salvation. But here I stand at the beginning of Lent, thinking about salvation, and here we stand at the beginning of Lent, thinking about salvation, and this is the question that scripture has called forth.

Who is blessed and who is cursed? Who is saved and who is condemned? Are some in and some out? Could it be that all are in? The lyrics of singer/songwriter Ani DiFranco come to mind. She sings "Their eyes are all asking me, 'are you in or are you out?' I think, 'oh man, what is this all about?'"

Indeed, we may wonder with Ani, what is this all about? God you say to Abraham that those who bless him will be blessed and the one who curses him will be cursed AND in him ALL the families of the earth will be blessed.

What is this all about? You speak through Christ of your wondrous love for the cosmos, for the universe, the love that willed salvation for that cosmos and not condemnation, BUT at the same time your underline the necessity of belief in Jesus Christ and birth in the Spirit. What is this all about?

A friend of mine once told me that he thought that after he studied the Bible diligently with a community of believers for seven years, he would have surely found answers to all of life's questions. But what he found instead was that he ended this seven years of study with MORE questions than when he began and thus, he went to seminary.

Here, in these passages of scripture we too find more questions than answers. We stand with Nicodemus puzzled, questioning. Nicodemus, a teacher of Israel, we, disciples of Christ, cannot understand.

John is an unambiguous gospel. If you look at the material immediately following today's passage you can see this. The question of who is in and who is out appears to be answered, if you believe in Christ you are already saved, if you do not believe you are already condemned. Perhaps it is tempting to say, 'See there is an answer in scripture if only we keep reading."

But I believe that if we CONTINUE to read, scripture ultimately keeps us questioning. For example, let's return our attention to Nicodemus. The Gospel of John may be unambiguous, but the character of Nicodemus in the Gospel of John is anything but. Is Nicodemus in or is he out? If this were the only mention of Nicodemus in all the gospel, we would probably be left with a pretty clear picture that he, the one who approached Jesus by night, was one of those whom John would call a lover of the darkness and not the light. He does not understand. He is included in the plural you of those who have not received the testimony of Christ and committed their hearts in belief. He does not believe. He is out.

Or is he? Nicodemus appears twice more in John's gospel. Mid-Gospel we see him step up to Jesus' defense advocating for a fair trial for Jesus when his fellow Pharisees were fighting to see Jesus thrown in jail. Currently his peers openly question him about where his allegiance lies. We are left wondering, with the Pharisees, where Nicodemus stands. Then, near the end of John's gospel he appears one more time. Now Jesus is dead, and Nicodemus joins Joseph of Arimathea in his burial preparations and he comes bearing a substantial gift of a hundred pounds of myrrh and aloe. The picture painted of Nicodemus is clearly quite ambiguous. Is he in or is he out?

There are suggestions of devotion to Christ in all three of these stories and these suggestions grow progressively stronger and speak progressively louder which suggests an evolution or transformation in his character. First, in the story we are considering today, Nicodemus approaches Jesus and honors him by acknowledging that he is one who has come from God. In the second story he defends Jesus at some potential risk to himself. In the third he offers an expensive and substantial gift to Jesus. What at first may seem clear becomes less and less clear as we continue to read and to reflect. So, is he in or is he out? What is this all about?

We, with Nicodemus, should not be astonished when we cannot understand. For Jesus speaks to us of mystery when he affirms that wind blows where it chooses and we hear it, but we do not know where it comes from or where it goes. We do not and cannot know where the spirit blows, how the spirit works, who is saved.

But we are here in church seeking to know, seeking to connect with Christ. We are on a quest for knowledge and understanding. On this quest, when we encounter uncertainty, ambiguity, and paradox, we are tempted to flatten what we find, to make it malleable, make it digestible, make it understandable. We are tempted to pick one dimension of a paradox and lift that dimension up as truth.

But on this quest for certain knowledge when we encounter scripture, we trip. When we encounter the cross and empty tomb, we stumble. When we encounter Jesus the Christ, we are stopped in our tracks. For the truth revealed in all these places, in these central elements of our faith is not the product of an either this/or that. It is a both this/and that. It is not simple and straightforward. It is paradox. And we cannot understand.

And it is exactly to this place of mystery, to this point of tension that I believe our scripture calls us today. We ask, 'is God's saving work in Christ for all or only for some?" And the answer we receive is somewhere in the middle. My leaning, and I suspect that it's the leaning of many, though surely not all, in this room, is to affirm that God's love is broad enough, deep enough, and wondrous enough to redeem ALL of creation. Whether you are poor or rich, whether you are educated or uneducated, whether you are straight or gay, whether you believe in Jesus or not. I want to believe that the God that I give my heart to is so wholly good and so powerful that all can and will be redeemed. And I can find support for this leaning in Genesis and John today. Did we not hear in Genesis that ALL the families of the earth would be blessed? Not just Jewish families. Not just prototypical middle-class American Protestant families with 2.5 kids, not just traditional families, ALL the families of the earth. And in John, we hear that God's love was for the cosmos and that God's intention was to save and not to condemn the cosmos, the whole universe. There is truly a message of universal potential in the words from God we have received today that could seem to make irrelevant the question of who is in and who is out.

But we would not be faithful if we limited our reading to that which confirms our leanings. There is a specific criterion for determination of who is in and who is out that is identified in John 3: 1-17. Belief in Christ is lifted up as crucial. Try as we might we cannot escape this clear message. This is an uncomfortable message for many of us as we seek to honestly engage the increasingly complex and pluralistic world in which live and in which we have been called to serve. Some leaders of interfaith movements suggest we speak more about God and less about Jesus to smooth out our relationships with our religious others. It is so tempting to focus on that which unites us to others as opposed to that which potentially divides us. But today's scripture does not allow us to make such a move. Belief in the very particular being of Jesus Christ is crucial.

In her book *Encountering God*, pluralist Diana Eck offers helpful reflections on the meaning of "belief". She shares that the word belief comes from the Old English, belove and thus that its original meaning reflects giving one's heart to something. Belief is not merely a matter of intellectual assent to a proposition, rather it is a matter of intimate relationship. And do we not know the power of intimate relationship? We see mothers nursing babes, and see that power revealed. We watch people fall in love, and see that power revealed. We connect with one another in Christian community, honoring our baptismal promises to guide and nurture one another, and feeding one another with God's own love and life, and we see the power of intimate relationship revealed. We know the power of intimate relationship. But can we even begin to fathom the power of intimate relationship with Jesus Christ? In the story of Nicodemus, we are offered a glimpse into the nearly unfathomable transformative potential of relationship with Christ. As Christians when we confess belief in Jesus Christ as Lord and Savior, as most of us have done and will likely do again, we express a trust and commitment that we too are willing to be transformed.

So, belief in Christ does matter. We cannot brush it aside. It is significant. But questions remain. Who is this Christ that we believe in? What is he all about? This very particular being is God's LOVE, GOD'S love, and as such is ultimately mystery. This very particular being ate with sinners and loved the unlovable. This very particular being challenged expectations. This very particular being died a gruesome death and then rose from the dead. This very particular being lives still and is our source of hope in a hopeless world. When I confess belief in the very particular being of Jesus Christ, it opens me to the universal potential of God's saving grace.

So, as we journey further into Lent, let us not seek to indulge our hunger for understanding; rather let us be fed by mystery. Let us not choose easy answers; rather, let us choose wonder. Who is in and who is out? Does Christ save some or does Christ save all? What is this all about? We cannot know. And we are not called to know. But we are called to believe. And we are called to be transformed by our belief. May we journey to the cross and beyond giving our hearts to Jesus the Christ.

Complicated Hearts
1 Samuel 16:1-13 (CEB); Psalm 51:10-14 (CEB)

This sermon was written for and delivered to St. Andrew's Presbyterian Church on Sunday, October 22, 2017. These were the narrative lectionary passages appointed for the day.

1 Samuel 16:1-13 (CEB)

> *1 The Lord said to Samuel, "How long are you going to grieve over Saul? I have rejected him as king over Israel. Fill your horn with oil and get going. I'm sending you to Jesse of Bethlehem because I have found my next king among his sons."*
>
> *2 "How can I do that?" Samuel asked. "When Saul hears of it, he'll kill me!"*
>
> *"Take a heifer with you," the Lord replied, "and say, 'I have come to make a sacrifice to the Lord.' 3 Invite Jesse to the sacrifice, and I will make clear to you what you should do. You will anoint for me the person I point out to you."*
>
> *4 Samuel did what the Lord instructed. When he came to Bethlehem, the city elders came to meet him. They were shaking with fear. "Do you come in peace?" they asked.*
>
> *5 "Yes," Samuel answered. "I've come to make a sacrifice to the Lord. Now make yourselves holy, then come with me to the sacrifice." Samuel made Jesse and his sons holy and invited them to the sacrifice as well.*
>
> *6 When they arrived, Samuel looked at Eliab and thought, that must be the Lord's anointed right in front.*
>
> *7 But the Lord said to Samuel, "Have no regard for his appearance or stature, because I haven't selected him. God doesn't look at things like humans do. Humans see only what is visible to the eyes, but the Lord sees into the heart."*
>
> *8 Next Jesse called for Abinadab, who presented himself to Samuel, but he said, "The Lord hasn't chosen this one either." 9 So Jesse presented Shammah, but Samuel said, "No, the Lord hasn't chosen this one." 10 Jesse presented seven of his sons to Samuel, but Samuel*

said to Jesse, "The Lord hasn't picked any of these." 11 Then Samuel asked Jesse, "Is that all of your boys?"

"There is still the youngest one," Jesse answered, "but he's out keeping the sheep."

"Send for him," Samuel told Jesse, "because we can't proceed until he gets here."

12 So Jesse sent and brought him in. He was reddish brown, had beautiful eyes, and was good-looking. The Lord said, "That's the one. Go anoint him." 13 So Samuel took the horn of oil and anointed him right there in front of his brothers. The Lord's spirit came over David from that point forward.

Then Samuel left and went to Ramah.

Psalm 51:10-14 (CEB)

10 Create a clean heart for me, God; put a new, faithful spirit deep inside me! 11 Please don't throw me out of your presence   please don't take your holy spirit away from me.

12 Return the joy of your salvation to me   and sustain me with a willing spirit. 13 Then I will teach wrongdoers your ways, and sinners will come back to you.

14 Deliver me from violence, God, God of my salvation, so that my tongue can sing of your righteousness.

***

I understand myself to be pretty people smart—one of my dominant forms of intelligence is the interpersonal. That said, I am utterly unable to see with clarity, and therefore to judge with any precision the heart of any other human being. By heart I mean inner being/soul/mind… the seat of discernment and decision making in each of us.

This limitation was revealed to me when I learned that a doctor I had trusted implicitly murdered his wife. In our four-year journey of trying to conceive a child, we worked with two different fertility specialists. The first had a beautiful office with pictures of gorgeous babies he had helped to bring into the world on all the walls. He was dripping with confidence, even bravado.

He told me I'd be pregnant in no time. I left meetings with him crying almost every time. I just didn't have a good feeling about this guy. My mom reminded me on her recent visit that, when, after several months I was still not pregnant, he questioned the strength of my faith. When I was still not pregnant a year later, I walked away from doctor number one. I spent a year trying to find peace and hope again. And then found doctor number two. Everything about him was humbler—his office space, his manner of speech. He was honest with me about his limitations and yet hopeful about possible outcomes for us. I was keeping a personal blog through this time and I labeled Doctor One-Dr. Night and Doctor Two-Dr. Day. It turned out that I didn't get pregnant with the help of either doctor. But I walked away from Dr. Day with wholly good feelings about his care.

I was pretty sure I could see the heart of these two guys. If you had told me that Dr. Night killed his wife, I'd be troubled but not surprised. But no, it was Dr. Day... gentle, humble Dr. Day... in jail now for murdering his wife and attempting to cover it up. So disturbing. So baffling. Did NOT see that coming. Apparently, I cannot see into the hearts of anybody—not clearly anyhow.

None of us can. Our first focal reading today suggests that only the Lord sees into human hearts, while acknowledging the limitation of human sight. Samuel wasn't interested in anointing another king. He hadn't wanted to anoint the first King of Israel—Saul. You see, Samuel, whom you met last week as a young boy, in today's story is an old man. And in the time that elapsed between his call in the temple and this story of the call and anointing of David he has not only been a prophet, but a judge of Israel—the last judge, in fact. By judge I don't mean an officer of the court—I mean a leader... the book of Judges is all about the period in Israel's history when they did not have a king, but instead leaders of different types rose up to help them when they went astray and were suffering/struggling. Among the judges were men and women, military heroes and prophets. And Samuel was the last. His sons, like his mentor Eli's sons, were disappointing and not able to continue his leadership and the people of Israel demanded a king. And as the story is told, God told Samuel to give them what they want, but to warn them that they would be disappointed. Samuel believed God alone should be king of Israel, but with God's guidance he anointed Saul, a tall, handsome, strong man as the first king of Israel.

But Saul fell out of favor with God, as the story is told, and gravely disappointed Samuel. At the beginning of our story today, Samuel is grieving the failures of Saul. And God tells Samuel to get up and get on with it—fill his horn and anoint the next King of Israel. God might have rejected Saul, but… he was still king. And Samuel knew that anointing a new king when another king was on the throne would likely result in a death sentence. God provides a way to mask what he is doing but doesn't remove the assignment from him. Samuel is to go to Bethlehem, find Jesse, and anoint one of his sons as king.

Jesse has eight sons. He somehow knows why Samuel is there—he presents seven of his sons, in order of age, before Samuel. Samuel is quite certain the oldest will be the king—he was impressive looking. And the first born had special standing culturally. But God redirects Samuel's attention—external appearance, cultural standing… these are human things… God sees into the heart. And Samuel systematically passes over each one of the seven sons lined up in front of him. In a Cinderella-like scene he asks if there is another… And Jesse acknowledges that the youngest is in the field keeping the sheep. Jesse never considered that his youngest son David could be called to so great a role. His vision is limited. But in fact, the one son that Jesse never considered, the one son Jesse couldn't see… he was the one. God pointed Samuel to this ruddy boy with beautiful eyes… this good-looking boy… but we're told that that's not the point—God pointed Samuel to this shepherd boy and told him to anoint him. And so, the baby of the family was anointed king right in front of all his brothers. And God's spirit filled him. Now, that verse about the Lord seeing into the heart might have us thinking that David, of all the eight brothers had the purest heart. But… if you read through the rest of 1st and 2nd Samuel it would be difficult for you to say this with any confidence. Do you know the story of David and Bathsheba? How he shirked his kingly duties and did not go to war with his troops? Took the wife of another man and raped her, impregnating her and then arranged to have her husband, a deeply loyal servant solider of the king killed in battle when he couldn't get the husband to go home to his wife to potentially cover up David's misdeed… I'm not making this up. You'll find it in your Bibles—2 Samuel 11. And there's an even worse story later—when one of David's sons rapes one of David's daughters… and David does NOTHING about it (2 Samuel 13).

Our second focal reading is a portion of a Psalm that the book of Psalms suggests was written by David after his grave sin with Bathsheba and her husband Uriah. If we go with this, we hear David praying for a clean heart… a new and faithful spirit deep within… David is praying that what happened to Saul—the withdrawal of God's Spirit, won't happen to him.

God knows David's heart. God knew it when David was chosen. God knows that David's heart was wounded by a father who couldn't see him and by a sitting king who, understandably, was deeply threatened by him. God knew the evil of which David was capable even before David knew. Hurt people hurt people.

God knows all our hearts. God knows that most of us, truly all of us, if we are humble enough to be honest, could pray the words of Psalm 51 at some time, or perhaps at several times in our lives. People of Judeo-Christian faith have found this to be a powerful prayer for confession for millennia. Every human being has a complicated heart. God can see this. It would be so much easier if some had good hearts and others evil. Really, if we're talking easier, how about everyone having purely good hearts? But my point is… we want to be able to sort the world into good and evil—to be able to trust certain people implicitly and distrust others implicitly, to categorize people into day and night. But as Jesus affirmed… no one is good but God alone. And, I would add, no one is evil… we all have complicated hearts that bear the capacity for good and evil, and everything in between.

It seems that, for some time, perhaps for all our history, but acutely for the last decade plus… in this country we have tended to try to sort our leaders into the categories of good or evil. Some thought our last president the Messiah incarnate, others thought him the devil. And… it seems we've just flipped it with our current president. The truth is that both Obama and Trump are human beings with complicated hearts that we cannot see. This is true of all human leaders… all have complicated hearts that we cannot see. So, we do well to pray for our leaders and to seek our ultimate guidance in the only source of true, uncomplicated goodness—God. And whenever we find ourselves being too certain about the heart of another, this is an invitation to remind ourselves who knows hearts and turn back to that one in humble faith.

Of This World/Not of This World
John 18:28-40 (CEB)

This sermon was written for and delivered to St. Andrew's Presbyterian Church on March 11, 2018, on a year four narrative lectionary passage, in the season of Lent. It is a response to one of the many mass shootings that have rocked our nation repeatedly.

John 18:28-40 (CEB)

> *28 The Jewish leaders led Jesus from Caiaphas to the Roman governor's palace. It was early in the morning. So that they could eat the Passover, the Jewish leaders wouldn't enter the palace; entering the palace would have made them ritually impure. 29 So Pilate went out to them and asked, "What charge do you bring against this man?"*
>
> *30 They answered, "If he had done nothing wrong, we wouldn't have handed him over to you."*
>
> *31 Pilate responded, "Take him yourselves and judge him according to your Law."*
>
> *The Jewish leaders replied, "The Law doesn't allow us to kill anyone." 32 This was so that Jesus' word might be fulfilled when he indicated how he was going to die.)*
>
> *32 Pilate went back into the palace. He summoned Jesus and asked, "Are you the king of the Jews?"*
>
> *33 Jesus answered, "Do you say this on your own or have others spoken to you about me?"*
>
> *34 Pilate responded, "I'm not a Jew, am I? Your nation and its chief priests handed you over to me. What have you done?"*
>
> *35 Jesus replied, "My kingdom doesn't originate from this world. If it did, my guards would fight so that I wouldn't have been arrested by the Jewish leaders. My kingdom isn't from here."*
>
> *36 "So you are a king?" Pilate said.*

Jesus answered, "You say that I am a king. I was born and came into the world for this reason: to testify to the truth. Whoever accepts the truth listens to my voice."

37 "What is truth?" Pilate asked.

After Pilate said this, he returned to the Jewish leaders and said, "I find no grounds for any charge against him. 39 You have a custom that I release one prisoner for you at Passover. Do you want me to release for you the king of the Jews?"

40 They shouted, "Not this man! Give us Barabbas!" (Barabbas was an outlaw.)

***

This week our state legislature became the first in the nation to pass a new gun law after the recent mass shooting at Marjorie Stoneman Douglas High School in Parkland, Florida. We may have been the first, but all eyes were on Florida, and a few days after Oregon legislators acted, the Florida State Legislature did. When I first drafted this sermon, it was uncertain whether the governor of Florida would sign the bill, but that he did, making this the first successful gun control measure passed in Florida in more than 20 years. And the activists who have emerged from the school shooting in Florida a month ago, many of them teenagers, are being given a lot of credit for this victory.

As is the case with most bills, the Florida gun bill is a mixed bag—it does some things, but not others. Here's what it does (according the NY times): it raises the minimum age for all gun purchases, creates a waiting period for most gun buyers, bans bump stocks, arms school employees, funds school security, and expands mental health services and regulations. Here's what it doesn't do (also according to the NY Times)—ban assault weapons, suspend AR-15 sales, ban high capacity magazines, strengthen background checks. It is a compromise. A mixed bag.

In America we cling tightly to our guns, in the name of our constitutional rights.

When mass shootings occur, nearly everyone cries out that something needs to be done. But we are sharply divided in our preferred responses. Some think it should be harder for civilians to get guns, and that certain guns should be taken out of circulation altogether. Others think more civilians should have guns and know how to use them. The bill passed in Florida this week seems to reflect both inclinations. While in some ways this law will make it harder for some people to get guns... the favorite weapons of mass shooters are left in circulation and more guns may be a regular presence in schools as a result of this legislation.

Florida's gun law is very much a plan of this world. In our world we regularly respond to violence with violence. I'm focusing on guns today, but I could talk about terrorism, or nuclear weaponry, or even trade... I could even talk about disputes between family and friends—violent words lead to punches thrown, to more violent words, to more violent acts. Violence begets violence. And so, it has long been. Our Gospel reading today testifies to this.

At the center of this portion of John's passion narrative, is the question of Jesus' kingship. Pilate asks Jesus, "Are you the King of the Jews?" Jesus doesn't deny this title, but he doesn't accept it either. Jesus is asked this question by Pilate in all four Gospels... it seems to be the basis for Rome to act against him. Is he a rival to the only king the Roman empire would accept, that being Caesar, the Roman emperor? Is he disturbing the peace in this territory of Rome? Are there any grounds for his execution? In all the Gospels the grounds are rather flimsy, in John they are non-existent. Those religious leaders who bring Jesus to Pilate don't even try to articulate a charge, they just make it clear they want Jesus dead. Pilate seems to try to find a reason and it all hangs on this question, "Are you the King of the Jews?" In the other three Gospels, Jesus replies tersely to this question, "You say so." But in this Gospel Jesus has a bit more to say... that is usually the case with this Gospel. Jesus, the Word made flesh, uses lots of words.

During Jesus' words spoken in response to this query we hear "My kingdom doesn't originate from this world. If it did, my guards would fight so that I wouldn't have been arrested by the Jewish leaders. My kingdom isn't from here." Jesus doesn't deny that he is a king... but he is *not* an earthly king. And why not? Because he responds non-violently, even in the face of violence. He says as much here. We didn't read the story of Jesus' arrest in the garden, perhaps you'll want to do that this afternoon, you'll find it earlier in this section, before the material we read last week. What you'll see is that, as John recalls it, Peter drew his sword to defend Jesus against those who came to arrest him. He even cut off the ear of a guard. But Jesus sternly admonished him, made him put his sword away. It seems that in God's kingdom there's no place for weapons and violence. Those are the tools of the kingdoms of this world, not of the kingdom of God.

So, I was shocked, in fact nauseated, by a set of images I found on Facebook, images of a worship service in which worshippers were holding assault rifles even as they lifted their hands in praise of God. One of the commenters called this idolatry, and that seemed spot on to me. If Jesus admonished Peter to put down his sword, would he not also have a stern word for followers today who pick up guns? When we choose to respond to violence by equipping ourselves for more violence we're playing by the rules of this world and forsaking the guidance of Jesus.

Yes, we have a right to bear arms in this country. Yes, there are better and worse uses of guns. Yes, it's what people do with guns that is the problem, guns in and of themselves are not inherently problematic. But... when guns are used to harm other people, as when Peter's sword was used to slice off an ear... this is not the way of Jesus. And it may seem that the way of Jesus is weakness in the face of strength, but Martin Luther King, Jr saw it differently. He saw great weakness in violence. He wrote *"The ultimate weakness of violence is that it is a descending spiral, begetting the very thing it seeks to destroy. Instead of diminishing evil, it multiplies it. Through violence you may murder the liar, but you cannot murder the lie, nor establish the truth. Through violence you may murder the hater, but you do not murder hate. In fact, violence merely increases hate. So, it goes. Returning violence for violence multiplies violence, adding deeper darkness to a night already devoid of stars. Darkness cannot drive out darkness: only light can do that. Hate cannot drive out hate: only love can do that."*

We are slowly working our way through the story of Jesus' passion according to John, through the story of his great suffering and then brutal and violent death. And all along the way we will see Jesus responding to violence, non-violently. In another Gospel he's recorded as saying from the cross, *'Father, forgive them, for they know not what they do."* Augustine, an early teacher of the church, suggested that it was Jesus' act of forgiveness extended to those who were killing him that led to so many being baptized that first Pentecost. *"Darkness cannot drive out darkness: only light can do that. Hate cannot drive out hate: only love can do that."* And it did. Ultimately, it is God who responds to the violence visited upon Jesus and God does so by granting life, resurrected life. That is a radically different response to violence than that which we most often muster in this world.

But sometimes we do manage to live in God's kingdom, even as we continue to navigate the vagaries of this earthly kingdom. I shared an article on Facebook recently, a lovely piece by Glennon Doyle, about a teacher who responded to Columbine... that school shooting in Colorado nearly 20 years ago... about a teacher who responded to this shooting by adopting a weekly practice in her fifth-grade classroom. I don't know that this teacher is a professing Christian. But I believe her response is a manifestation of the power of God's Spirit opening different possibilities not of this world, during our world. Allow me to share excerpts of her essay—

> *"Every Friday afternoon, she asks her students to take out a piece of paper and write down the names of four children with whom they'd like to sit the following week. The children know that these requests may or may not be honored. She also asks the students to nominate one student who they believe has been an exceptional classroom citizen that week. All ballots are privately submitted to her.*
>
> *"And every single Friday afternoon, after the students go home, she takes out those slips of paper, places them in front of her, and studies them. She looks for patterns. Who is not getting requested by anyone else? Who can't think of anyone to request? Who never gets noticed enough to be nominated? Who had a million friends last week and none this week?*
>
> *"... [This teacher] isn't looking for a new seating chart or "exceptional citizens." She's looking for lonely children. She's looking for children struggling to connect with other children. She's identifying the little ones who are falling through the cracks of the class' social life. She is discovering whose gifts are going unnoticed by their peers. And she's pinning down—right away—who's being bullied and who is doing the bullying.*
>
> *"...This brilliant woman watched Columbine knowing that all violence begins with disconnection. All outward violence begins as inner loneliness. Who are our next mass shooters and how do we stop them? She watched that tragedy knowing that children who aren't being noticed may eventually resort to being noticed by any means necessary."*

This teacher translated her distress over blood spilled so unnecessarily into action to reduce the likelihood that kids who pass through her classroom will ever be so desperate as to resort to great violence. She met darkness with light, hatred with love. And friends, I believe we all need to find ways to do the same, to bring thoughts, prayers, and action together. A great way to do this would be to send a strong St. Andrew's contingent to the Portland installment of the March for Our Lives on Saturday, March 24th. This is the day before Holy Week, our week for intense meditation on Jesus' journey into Jerusalem and to his death on the cross. Let us stand in solidarity with students who are non-violently responding to the violence too regularly visited upon them, bringing a steady call for action that will further life and not death. Please let me know if you are interested in joining me in bearing witness on the 24th.

As one pastor put it *"after our praying, we are called to witness: to witness to the One who demonstrated power through weakness, who manifested strength through vulnerability, who established justice through mercy, and who built the kingdom of God by embracing a confused, chaotic, and violent world, taking its pain into his own body, dying the death it sought, and rising again to remind us that light is stronger than darkness, love is stronger than hate, and that with God, all good things are possible."*

Information about sources that were cited in or that informed this sermon:

I learned about the Oregon gun law passed this week via this site: http://thehill.com/homenews/state-watch/376893-oregon-becomes-first-state-to-add-new-gun-law-since-parkland-shooting

The information about the Florida gun law was derived from this article: https://www.nytimes.com/2018/03/08/us/florida-gun-bill.html

Martin Luther King Quote from *"Where Do We Go from Here?"* as published in Where Do We Go from Here: Chaos or Community? (1967), p. 62 and quoted in http://

www.davidlose.net/2015/11/christ-the-king-b-not-of-this-world/ from which the final quote in the sermon is also taken.

The story about the teacher can be read in full at this site: http://momastery.com/blog/2014/01/30/share-schools/

Being Seen
Luke 7:36-8:3 (NRSV)

This sermon/dramatic monologue was originally written for the First Presbyterian Church of Lowville, NY, but I have delivered it in multiple congregations, most memorably in the Village Church in Nashville, TN. I always memorize my monologue sermons and deliver them from the floor.

Luke 7:36-8:3 (NRSV)

36 One of the Pharisees asked Jesus to eat with him, and he went into the Pharisee's house and took his place at the table. 37 And a woman in the city, who was a sinner, having learned that he was eating in the Pharisee's house, brought an alabaster jar of ointment. 38 She stood behind him at his feet, weeping, and began to bathe his feet with her tears and to dry them with her hair. Then she continued kissing his feet and anointing them with the ointment. 39 Now when the Pharisee who had invited him saw it, he said to himself, "If this man were a prophet, he would have known who and what kind of woman this is who is touching him—that she is a sinner." 40 Jesus spoke up and said to him, "Simon, I have something to say to you." "Teacher," he replied, "speak." 41 "A certain creditor had two debtors; one owed five hundred denarii, and the other fifty. 42 When they could not pay, he canceled the debts for both. Now which of them will love him more?" 43 Simon answered, "I suppose the one for whom he canceled the greater debt." And Jesus said to him, "You have judged rightly." 44 Then turning toward the woman, he said to Simon, "Do you see this woman? I entered your house; you gave me no water for my feet, but she has bathed my feet with her tears and dried them with her hair. 45 You gave me no kiss, but from the time I came in she has not stopped kissing my feet. 46 You did not anoint my head with oil, but she has anointed my feet with ointment. 47 Therefore, I tell you, her sins, which were many, have been forgiven; hence she has shown great love. But the one to whom little is forgiven, loves little." 48 Then he said to her, "Your sins are forgiven." 49 But those who were at the table with him began to say among themselves, "Who is this who even forgives sins?" 50 And he said to the woman, "Your faith has saved you; go in peace."

8 Soon afterwards he went on through cities and villages, proclaiming and bringing the good news of the kingdom of God. The twelve were with him, 2 as well as some women who had been cured of evil spirits and infirmities: Mary, called Magdalene, from whom seven demons had gone out, 3 and Joanna, the wife of Herod's steward Chuza, and Susanna, and many others, who provided for them out of their resources.

***

He saw me. He looked right at me and he really saw me-me, the real me. And he loved me anyhow.

Until the day I met him I spent so much energy trying to disappear, trying to make myself invisible. I couldn't bear the whispering, the clucking, the catty comments, the stern looks of disapproval. I hated myself for the mistakes I had made, the harm I had done, and the harm that had been done to me. And usually when people looked at me all they could see was my sin and what I saw reflected in their eyes made me sick. And so, I tried to disappear, to be inconspicuous, to fade out of view. And soon, people stopped seeing me altogether. I pulled in and blended in so effectively, I did disappear.

I stopped even being able to really see myself. Until he saw me.

When he looked at me, I knew he was seeing ALL OF ME. The whole truth about me. He was seeing me. And he didn't turn away disgusted. He didn't cluck or comment. He just looked at me, with love, with deep and fierce love. And I was the one who turned away. My face flushed under the intensity of his gaze, my gut quivered at the thought that he could see me and that he could love me. He was just a man, or so I thought at the time, but something about the way he looked at me told me that God loves me, the real me, and God forgives me. And this knowledge was too much for me. It didn't make sense. How could a man I've never met, know me so completely, and love me anyhow? How could God love me and forgive me when I cannot love and forgive myself? I turned away, face burning with shame, as if I had been stripped naked before him. I turned and walked away.

I went home and sat down in front of my mirror and tried to see myself as he had seen me. But I could not look at myself with the love with which he had looked at me. All I could see was how broken I am. All I could see in that mirror was a woman who had strayed so far from the path she imagined she would travel when she was a young girl. When I thought of the joy that had filled me as a child, the sense of hope and possibility that had propelled my young frame forward and contrasted that with the shrinking violet I had become, the burdened, disappearing disappointment I was, I began to weep. I saw in the mirror a broken and hurting woman and I wept all the harder. I wept for all the mistakes I had made. I wept for all I had lost. I wept for all my failings. I wept for all the years I had spent disappearing.

I had not wept like this since my mother died. And without thinking I became as I was upon her death. I took my hair down out of it's neat binding, I removed my sandals, I wore my grief for all to see. No one around me could understand why I was dressed for death when no one had died. No one could grasp where my weeping was coming from. No one could see me, really see me. I needed to get back to the one who could see me, who had seen me, and to the one who could love me, who did love me. I could not accept then that I was accepted, grieving as I was my faults and failings, but I needed to get back to that man who had looked at me with such love. I needed to be near him again. I needed to thank him, but I also just needed him.

I grabbed the most precious jar of ointment in the house and stumbled out into the twilight of that night. I went to where I had seen him last, but he wasn't there. I fell to my knees and wept all the harder. When I grew too tired to weep anymore, I just sat on the ground, my hair disheveled, my heart heavy, and the I heard someone say "Why do you suppose Simon invited Jesus over to dinner tonight? I thought the Pharisees had a problem with Jesus." I jumped up and headed straight for Simon's home. Everyone knows where Simon lives, he's one of the most prominent men in town. I'd never been inside before. It was quite clear that I was not welcome there. And I hadn't wanted to be out in public all that much anyhow. I knew that I didn't belong there that night even, but I had to be with Jesus. I had to be with the man who had seen me. I had to get close to him. I had to thank him. I needed him to see me again, to help me see me differently.

So, I ran there. It was a hot and sticky night, so the door was open to allow a breeze to blow through. I could hear quite a lot of noise coming from inside. It was clearly quite a dinner party. When I looked in through the door, I saw men reclining at table, obviously contented after a large meal. My heart sank as I could not see Jesus, but then a man with his back to the door turned just slightly, he caught sight of me out of the corner of his eye and I was pulled by a force I can't quite explain into the room. Only him took any notice of me, the invisible woman. I stood behind him and being so near to this one who could see me and love me anyhow... I started to weep again. The laughter and reverie of the party was so loud that no one could hear me. But I was weeping uncontrollably. I lowered my head trying to be as inconspicuous as possible, old habits die hard, and I looked down and saw that my tears were falling on his feet, feet which were filthy from the miles he had walked that day. I feel prostrate at his feet, now damp with my tears, and my loose hair draped over his feet and legs. I shocked myself then by taking his feet in my hands and using my hair as a towel to dry them, and then I remembered why I had come, and I reached for my alabaster jar broke it open and poured the oil on those feet. I rubbed his feet and then was overcome and started to kiss them. I kissed them repeatedly.

I was completely absorbed in this act of showing love to the one who first loved me, so I didn't realize that when Jesus started teaching Simon about debts and love that he was talking about me. I didn't know he was talking about me until he said, "Do you see this woman?" I almost laughed at this question. Of course, no one saw me, but then I felt all eyes on me as he began to celebrate what I had just done, as he compared me to Simon and made me look so good. And then he said out loud what I had known in my heart-my sins have been forgiven. He said it out loud, in front of all those people, my sins have been forgiven. I have been forgiven. And then he turned and looked right at me, he looked at me again, and with such love, he saw me, truly saw me and said to me "Your sins are forgiven." Everyone in the room was looking at him now, but he was looking at me, so intensely, when he spoke of my salvation when he tried to send me away with peace.

He did give me peace, but I had no intention of going far from him. I needed to stay near to him. I joined the band of women and men who followed him wherever he went. I needed to stay near to this one who could see me. I needed to stay close to this one who had forgiven me. I needed to hear of this forgiveness repeatedly. It's not that I don't believe it. But I have a hard time remembering it, and so I follow, every day, I follow.

Can you see yourself?

This monologue was inspired by a careful reading of the Gospel text for this week and was significantly influenced by the following article:

Cosgrove, Charles H. (2005). "A Woman's Unbound Hair in the Greco-Roman World, with Special Reference to the 'Sinful Woman' in Luke 7:36-50" in the *Journal of Biblical Literature*. Found on-line at http://www.sbl-site.org/Publications/JBL/JBL1244.pdf

Do You Believe This?
John 11:1-45 (NRSV)

This sermon/dramatic monologue was originally written for and delivered to the First Presbyterian Church of Lowville, NY on March 13, 2005. I have delivered it a few times since. Again, I deliver it memorized, from the floor.

John 11:1-45 (NRSV)

11 Now a certain man was ill, Lazarus of Bethany, the village of Mary and her sister Martha. 2 Mary was the one who anointed the Lord with perfume and wiped his feet with her hair; her brother Lazarus was ill. 3 So the sisters sent a message to Jesus, "Lord, he whom you love is ill." 4 But when Jesus heard it, he said, "This illness does not lead to death; rather it is for God's glory, so that the Son of God may be glorified through it." 5 Accordingly, though Jesus loved Martha and her sister and Lazarus, 6 after having heard that Lazarus was ill, he stayed two days longer in the place where he was.

7 Then after this he said to the disciples, "Let us go to Judea again." 8 The disciples said to him, "Rabbi, the Jews were just now trying to stone you, and are you going there again?" 9 Jesus answered, "Are there not twelve hours of daylight? Those who walk during the day do not stumble, because they see the light of this world. 10 But those who walk at night stumble, because the light is not in them." 11 After saying this, he told them, "Our friend Lazarus has fallen asleep, but I am going there to awaken him." 12 The disciples said to him, "Lord, if he has fallen asleep, he will be all right." 13 Jesus, however, had been speaking about his death, but they thought that he was referring merely to sleep. 14 Then Jesus told them plainly, "Lazarus is dead. 15 For your sake I am glad I was not there, so that you may believe. But let us go to him." 16 Thomas, who was called the Twin, said to his fellow disciples, "Let us also go, that we may die with him."

17 When Jesus arrived, he found that Lazarus had already been in the tomb four days. 18 Now Bethany was near Jerusalem, some two miles away, 19 and many of the Jews had come to Martha and Mary to console them about their brother. 20 When Martha heard that Jesus was coming, she went and met him, while Mary stayed at home. 21 Martha said to Jesus, "Lord, if you had been here, my brother would not have died. 22 But even now I know that God will give you whatever you ask of him." 23 Jesus said to her, "Your brother will rise again."

24 Martha said to him, "I know that he will rise again in the resurrection on the last day." 25 Jesus said to her, "I am the resurrection and the life. Those who believe in me, even though they die, will live, 26 and everyone who lives and believes in me will never die. Do you believe this?" 27 She said to him, "Yes, Lord, I believe that you are the Messiah, the Son of God, the one coming into the world."

28 When she had said this, she went back and called her sister Mary, and told her privately, "The Teacher is here and is calling for you." 29 And when she heard it, she got up quickly and went to him. 30 Now Jesus had not yet come to the village but was still at the place where Martha had met him. 31 The Jews who were with her in the house, consoling her, saw Mary get up quickly and go out. They followed her because they thought that she was going to the tomb to weep there. 32 When Mary came where Jesus was and saw him, she knelt at his feet and said to him, "Lord, if you had been here, my brother would not have died." 33 When Jesus saw her weeping, and the Jews who came with her also weeping, he was greatly disturbed in spirit and deeply moved. 34 He said, "Where have you laid him?" They said to him, "Lord, come and see." 35 Jesus began to weep. 36 So the Jews said, "See how he loved him!" 37 But some of them said, "Could not he who opened the eyes of the blind man have kept this man from dying?"

38 Then Jesus, again greatly disturbed, came to the tomb. It was a cave, and a stone was lying against it. 39 Jesus said, "Take away the stone." Martha, the sister of the dead man, said to him, "Lord, already there is a stench because he has been dead four days." 40 Jesus said to her, "Did I not tell you that if you believed, you would see the glory of God?" 41 So they took away the stone. And Jesus looked upward and said, "Father, I thank you for having heard me. 42 I knew that you always hear me, but I have said this for the sake of the crowd standing here, so that they may believe that you sent me." 43 When he had said this, he cried with a loud voice, "Lazarus, come out!" 44 The dead man came out, his hands and feet bound with strips of cloth, and his face wrapped in a cloth. Jesus said to them, "Unbind him, and let him go."

45 Many of the Jews therefore, who had come with Mary and had seen what Jesus did, believed in him.

Lazarus was ill, very ill. We had never seen him so ill before. I had nursed him through illnesses, placed cold cloths on his head through fevers, brought him cool water to sip countless times before, but this time, nothing Mary or I did make any difference.

He grew paler and paler, weaker and weaker, sicker and sicker, we could feel death lingering at the door. There was nothing left to do, but to call our beloved friend, Jesus. He was our only hope. He had been healing the sick for months now, why we even heard that he restored the sight of a man born blind, he could help our brother. And he knew and loved our brother, surely, he would come and make him well again, for he had helped even strangers in the past.

So, we sent word 'Lord, he whom you love is ill." We felt better as soon as we sent the message. The worrying, the fretting, the occasional tears of the days just past, all faded away as we confidently waited for Jesus. I continued to attend to Lazarus, but I hummed and even laughed a little as I did, for I knew Jesus was on his way. The first day was a day of joyful anticipation. The second day Lazarus stopped talking to us, he was breathing, but his breath was shallow and labored. He wouldn't open his eyes. I kept opening the front door and looking outside and straining to see Jesus approaching with his disciples. But I could see nothing. Mary sat, staring out the window. And then he died. I came back from checking for Jesus and I noticed he wasn't breathing any longer. That was it. Jesus never came. And he died.

We crashed so quickly from our height of hope for Lazarus' recovery, to the depth of devastation at his death. The ache was dreadful. He died too soon and so unnecessarily. If Jesus had only been there. Mary and I wrapped his body in strips of cloth, his face in a cloth. And then the men of our family carried him to the cave and laid him in it. Prayers were said. But I could not hear them through my sobs. The thud of the stone being rolled over the entrance to the caves jolted me, and I began to wail. Four days we spent inside the house or outside his tomb weeping and mourning. Friends and family from Jerusalem kept coming to cry with us, to try to feed us, to accompany us to our visits to the tomb. By the third day I couldn't cry any more. My sadness had hardened to anger. Jesus was still not there. Some friend. Some man of God.

On the fourth day I sat beside the window with a vacant stare. Mary was crying on her bed. All our visitors were in trying to comfort her. I saw someone running towards our house and I jumped up and opened the door. 'Jesus is coming!" They declared between gasps of breath. I don't know what came over me, but I tore out of the house and went and found him on the road. I hadn't been out of the house, save for trips to the tomb, in days. I wasn't supposed to leave the house save for trips to the tomb, but I had to go to him. The closer I came to him, the sorrow and anger within me revived and intensified. The words came hurtling out of me, the words I had been turning over and over in my head for days, as soon as I stood in front of him. 'Lord, if you had been here, my brother would not have died."

But then I looked in his eyes. Then I remembered who I was talking to. I saw such compassion in his eyes, compassion I had longed for days. I knew he knew my pain and I knew he felt it. I knew he was still a faithful friend. I knew he was still a man of God. The next words out of my mouth were calmer, and they surprised even me 'But even now I know God will give you whatever you ask of him." I don't know what I wanted Jesus to ask God, for my comfort I suppose and for Mary's, for relief from the ache of this loss. I knew it didn't matter what I wanted, Jesus would take care of me. He said to me so confidently, so compassionately, "Your brother will rise again." These words were comforting, they reminded me of my faith that new life would be granted on the last day, I confessed, 'I know that he will rise again in the resurrection on the last day." And I will never forget what he said next 'I am the resurrection and the life. Those who believe in me, even though they die, will live, and everyone who lives and believes in me will never die. Do you believe this?" Chills ran down my spine. He asked me so earnestly if I believed, and in that moment, I knew that I did. My disappointment, my sorrow, my anger was all still there, but a peace, a peace I can't even begin to describe, came over me. I looked in his eyes as he waited for my reply, and I gave my heart to him completely "Yes, Lord, I believe that you are the Messiah, the Son of God, the one coming into the world." My brother may have died. I knew that Mary and I would die someday too. But I knew that all would be well for I was standing in front of our long-awaited savior and he was promising life beyond death.

He took me in his arms and held me awhile, then he asked me to go get Mary. And so, I did. I calmly walked back home, went into her room where she was still crying on her bed, and quietly said to her "The Teacher is here and is calling for you." I recognized the urgency with which she leapt out of bed and stumbled towards the door. She was still sobbing, and all our visitors followed her, thinking she was going to the tomb. She found Jesus right where I found him, fell on her knees, and blurted out the same words I had blurted out 'Lord, if you had been here my brother would not have died." And then she collapsed in sobs. Everyone around her started crying more loudly then too.

Jesus looked at her huddled on the ground shaking as she sobbed and the look on his face was one of profound pain. I had never seen him so distressed. "Where have you laid him?" He asked. Friends stood on either side of Mary and lifted her up, and everyone gathered said *"Lord, come and see."* And then Jesus began to weep, deep, deep cries, gigantic tears dropped to the ground. The weeping crowd leaned into each other and all made their way to the tomb. We stood in front of the cave with the large stone rolled in front of it. And Jesus choked out *"Take away the stone."* I didn't know why he didn't just give the others the good news he had given me. It had brought me peace. It would surely do the same for them. Why should we roll away the stone and reveal his rotting, stinking body? He had been dead for four days, his soul had long since left him. He was dead. We should leave the dead to rest. I told Jesus as much *"Lord, already there is a stench because he has been dead four days."* He looked at me, tears rolling down his face, *"Did I not tell you that if you believed you would see the glory of God?"* And as he spoke, I heard his earlier words *"Your brother will rise again."* And I heard my earlier words *"I believe. You are the Messiah, the Son of God, the one coming into the world."* I stepped aside as two men rolled away the stone.

Jesus looked towards heaven and prayed, prayed that others would come to believe. I said a silent prayer with him. And then he cried out in a loud voice *"Lazarus, come out!"* All gasped, I nearly fainted, when a moment later he walked out of the tomb, all wrapped in cloths. He was alive. My brother who was dead, was alive again, by the power of God, through the love of Jesus. He was alive! I hadn't dared to even ask for this and yet my deepest prayer had been answered. For days I had been clinging to death, for years I had been clinging to death. On that day I embraced life. Never again will I cling to death, for I believe. I believe. I believe. Do you?

Section Three

Being Who God Calls Us to Be

Dancing Prophet
Exodus 3:1-12 (NRSV)

This is a sermon that has had many incarnations. I first wrote the story with which it begins for a phenomenology exercise in the Introduction to Theology class at McCormick Theological Seminary.

I worked it into a sermon on Exodus 3 for First Presbyterian Church of Lowville sometime early in my call there and have reworked it several times.

This version is the most recent revision written for my neutral pulpit for my call to St. Andrew's Presbyterian Church on inauguration weekend in January 2017.

Exodus 3:1-12 (NRSV)

> *3 Moses was keeping the flock of his father-in-law Jethro, the priest of Midian; he led his flock beyond the wilderness, and came to Horeb, the mountain of God. 2 There the angel of the Lord appeared to him in a flame of fire out of a bush; he looked, and the bush was blazing, yet it was not consumed. 3 Then Moses said, "I must turn aside and look at this great sight and see why the bush is not burned up." 4 When the Lord saw that he had turned aside to see, God called to him out of the bush, "Moses, Moses!" And he said, "Here I am." 5 Then he said, "Come no closer! Remove the sandals from your feet, for the place on which you are standing is holy ground." 6 He said further, "I am the God of your father, the God of Abraham, the God of Isaac, and the God of Jacob." And Moses hid his face, for he was afraid to look at God.*
>
> *7 Then the Lord said, "I have observed the misery of my people who are in Egypt; I have heard their cry on account of their taskmasters. Indeed, I know their sufferings, 8 and I have come down to deliver them from the Egyptians, and to bring them up out of that land to a good and broad land, a land flowing with milk and honey, to the country of the Canaanites, the Hittites, the Amorites, the Perizzites, the Hivites, and the Jebusites. 9 The cry of the Israelites has now come to me; I have also seen how the Egyptians oppress them. 10 So come, I will send you to Pharaoh to bring my people, the Israelites, out of Egypt." 11 But Moses said to God, "Who am I that I should go to Pharaoh, and bring the Israelites out of Egypt?" 12 He said, "I will be with you; and this shall be the sign for you that it is I who sent you: when*

you have brought the people out of Egypt, you shall worship God on this mountain."

***

I grew up in Syracuse, New York. There's a popular barbeque joint in my hometown called the Dinosaur Barbeque. On nearly any day at lunchtime or dinnertime the Dinosaur nearly bursts at the seams; it fills with an eclectic mix of people who eagerly devour scrumptious plates piled high with a host of meats in savory sauces and the best assortment of side dishes available anywhere in Central New York. But after dark, the Dinosaur is a different scene. When the sun goes down the mix of people stays eclectic but changes dramatically. Motorcycles line up outside, and people pour off these bikes and into the Dinosaur for what is reputed to be some of the best Blues music in Central New York.

When I returned to Syracuse after my graduation from college, now an adult with full access to all the haunts of my hometown, I must admit I found myself a wee bit intimidated by the Dinosaur after dark. I preferred to dine there at dusk in the well-lit front room. But one night my friend Alisha talked me into joining the biker crowd to listen to her friend's band play.

We were both newcomers to the Dinosaur at night and we had no idea what we would encounter. And as our wheels were not a Harley, but rather a Chevy Cavalier, we feared we would stick out like sore thumbs. We made nervous preparations for the evening. We planned our outfits carefully, parked SEVERAL blocks away, and slid into the last open booth, close to the door, in the room where the band was supposed to be playing. Despite our careful preparations and calculations, we felt incredibly conspicuous. We didn't even know where to focus our gaze as we didn't know where the stage was, and the band was nowhere to be seen. We sat there cautiously scanning the room for several minutes and swapping observations now and then.

Finally, music erupted behind us and it provided us instant relief. Now we had a reason to be there. The music was so lively and so powerful that we couldn't help but move in our seats. After a few minutes Alisha's mouth dropped open and she said 'Sarah, look!" I whipped around to see a woman--dancing—ALONE—in front of the band. To say that she was dancing doesn't quite capture the moment. To get a sense of this moment, picture a five-year-old girl who has just discovered pop music, flailing in her living room to her favorite new song on the radio. I mean, this woman was ALL over the place. Her arms and legs were going different directions. At times her kicks rivaled the Rockettes. She was like a ball of fire. Alisha and I just sat there gaping in a stunned silence. We couldn't believe that anyone would dance like THAT, ALONE, in front of all those people. We hoped it was alcohol leading her to this foolishness. We really wished we could put out her fire. We were embarrassed for her. Her solo flailing continued for a few songs, but eventually a few others joined her, and after six or seven songs the dance floor was full. Alisha and I stayed in our seats now in awe of what we had just witnessed.

Then to our surprise, or perhaps more accurately, to our horror, the dancing woman exited the dance floor and made a bee line for OUR booth. She threw her purse on the table and plopped down next to ME. Before Alisha and I could even exchange "What on earth is she doing?" glances, she blurted out "You girls are so cute. Why aren't you dancing?" Alisha instantly replied, "I don't dance. But SHE dances." My face went red and I stammered out some half-truth like "Oh, I'm just not in the mood for dancing." The truth is my body was dying to spring forth and embrace the music, but my mind was unwilling to run the risk of being watched as I had been watching her. By this time, we ascertained that this wild woman was not drunk; she was just different. She took a good, hard look at us both and said "You can't waste music man. You just can't waste the music." After rifling through her purse on an unsuccessful search for lipstick she disappeared into the thick, dancing crowd.

I never did dance that night, but I couldn't get her words out of my head. I kept asking myself "Do I waste music?" In time, my embarrassment was more for me than for her. "Do I waste music?" I'm sure she had no idea what her words would mean to me. This night, several years back, is probably not even a blip on her radar screen. But for me, to this day, she is the dancing prophet. Her declaration changed the way I thought about a whole host of things. She made me see myself differently. The dancing prophet challenged my expectations and left me feeling a bit uncomfortable. The dancing prophet was my burning bush and voice of God calling me to a new, less inhibited, freer, way of life. Through her, God beckoned me to come alive.

I think I know how Moses must have felt. Moses was at once doing something very familiar and exploring somewhere unfamiliar. He was keeping the flock, that was his daily work, but he was 'beyond the wilderness". This expression beyond the wilderness is like the far, far away or deep in the forest of fairy tales. He was in a slightly fantastical setting, near, of all places, the mountain of God. He probably had a sense that things weren't quite normal. He probably was a little nervous, but excited too. Then he saw a bush burning, but not burning up and he was mystified. He stared at this burning bush. He just couldn't get his head around what he was seeing.

I picture Moses, mouth gaping, not unlike our wide mouthed stares at the flailing, dancing prophet. In the Bible fire is a symbol of passion, of purity, of light, of mystery. And, it is extinguishable.

Seeing the sight of a burning, but not burning up, bush is enough to awe and mystify, but it is just the attention getter really. Some may see their burning bushes and know what to do. Most, I think, need a little more instruction. Moses did. So, God started talking through the bush. As if a bush that is burning, but not burned up is not wonder enough, now we have a talking bush. And it is through the words of God through this fiery bush that Moses gets his call. Moses is called by God to a new way of life. Set aside the familiar. Go back to Egypt (from where he had previously run for his life). And set my people free. This is not a comfortable call. God challenged all the expectations Moses had of leading a relatively quiet life with his wife caring for his father-in-law's flocks. God made Moses uncomfortable, by calling him way out of his comfort zone to take on a task that he could hardly fathom. That's just like God. Bushes don't just burn, and dancing prophets don't just dance. They talk. Inviting work for liberation-perhaps of a people, perhaps of ourselves. What seems drunk and crazy, is sober and wise. What seems a mere curiosity, grabs hold of you and makes a claim on your life. What seems inconsequential turns out to be a word from God.

Now Moses did not jump at the opportunity to run back to Egypt and save God's people. No, he had four objections to raise before he went forth. We only hear two of those objections in the part of the story we read this morning. But Moses stands back and practically scoffs at God's suggestion four times. First he says "Who am I to do this?? What are my qualifications?" Then "No one will believe me because I don't know the name of the God for whom I speak." Then "No one will believe that God chose ME." Then "I don't speak well. You can't mean me." The bush is burning in front of him and talking and all he can do is look for a bucket. Confronted with an unnerving talking bush in the wilderness or a dancing prophet in a booth, the tendency is to want to snuff out the fire, make it go away. "Just let me tend my sheep, you can't really want me."

But the thing is, God has essentially one response to all the objections that Moses can muster. "Don't worry about it. I will be with you." When God says that God's name is "I am who I am" this is an affirmation of God's presence and reality.

When God gives Moses the power to work miracles to convince the people of his call, this is a sign of God's presence with Moses. And when Moses says he can't speak well enough to do this job, God says "I'll take care of it. I'll be with you. Don't worry about it." There's no substantial point, counter point here. God has one point. I am calling you and I will be with you.

Neither God nor God's call go away if they're for real. God dances, burns, pokes, prods, whispers, sings to us—to not waste the music of our lives with insecurities and fears. When we know God to be with us, we can overcome fear.

Fear. There's plenty of that circulating in our nation and world right now, no? This moment in history when a highly controversial and to some, deeply troubling, man has just been inaugurated as our president, after a year in which we've watched with horror as numerous people of color have lost their lives at the hands of people sworn to protect us and numerous police officers have lost their lives in a backlash of rage, when weather events are getting more intense and the consequences devastating as the global temperature rises, as so many people worldwide and even right here in Portland are living in desperate poverty, as hate crimes escalate in the wake of a brutal electoral season. You might say that our nation is burning right now, and God is surely speaking, calling us to participate in liberation of people and this planet.

It all can feel like just too much, can't it? It's tempting to hunker down and watch another episode on Netflix, to tune out because it's painful to tune in. But as a friend of mine shared eloquently on Facebook the day before the election… no matter the results of the election, after a bit of grieving it will be time to roll up our sleeves and get to work.

If you're feeling scared and uncomfortable right now, you might just be close to call. Moses was scared and uncomfortable when called to confront the powers that be, was he not?

So where is the music playing in your life—the music that makes you want to dance, but, for fear, you're holding back? What gifts has God given you that our world needs right now? Don't waste the music. I once heard a professor say that if Jesus Christ has indeed been raised from the dead then the only appropriate response is dancing. He then leaned in and asked, "How are your churches doing with the dancing?" Jesus Christ has been raised from the dead, your sins have been forgiven, and maybe there really is nothing to do but dance. And by dance… I mean joyfully serve, and if you happen to get your groove on in the meantime, great! Goodness knows our Presbyterian churches could benefit from a bit of actual dancing now and then!

When we get engaged with what God is up to in the world, we're dancing and not wasting the music of our lives. When we increase our commitment to and engagement in the ministries of our churches, we're dancing and not wasting the music of our lives. When we use the gifts, we've been given to build up the body of Christ in the world, we're dancing and not wasting the music of our lives. When we gather for worship to sing praise, to hear God's word proclaimed, to gather at font and table, God is with us, in us, renewing us, empowering us to joyfully respond to God's call on our lives. We say, "You can't mean me." God says, "I am with YOU and I mean YOU." We say, "I don't have what it takes." God says "I'm what it takes. You have me. Let's dance."

Irresistible Grace
Jonah 3:1-5, 10 (NRSV); Mark 1:14-20 (NRSV)

This is a revision of a sermon originally written for First Presbyterian Church of Lowville, NY. This version was delivered at First Presbyterian Church of Lebanon, Tennessee during my seven months as a transitional supply pastor there.

Jonah 3:1-5, 10 (NRSV)

> 3 The word of the Lord came to Jonah a second time, saying, 2 "Get up, go to Nineveh, that great city, and proclaim to it the message that I tell you." 3 So Jonah set out and went to Nineveh, according to the word of the Lord. Now Nineveh was an exceedingly large city, a three days' walk across. 4 Jonah began to go into the city, going a day's walk. And he cried out, "Forty days more, and Nineveh shall be overthrown!" 5 And the people of Nineveh believed God; they proclaimed a fast, and everyone, great and small, put on sackcloth.
>
> 10 When God saw what they did, how they turned from their evil ways, God changed his mind about the calamity that he had said he would bring upon them; and he did not do it.

Mark 1:14-20 (NRSV)

> 14 Now after John was arrested, Jesus came to Galilee, proclaiming the good news of God, 15 and saying, "The time is fulfilled, and the kingdom of God has come near; repent, and believe in the good news."
>
> 16 As Jesus passed along the Sea of Galilee, he saw Simon and his brother Andrew casting a net into the sea—for they were fishermen. 17 And Jesus said to them, "Follow me and I will make you fish for people." 18 And immediately they left their nets and followed him. 19 As he went a little farther, he saw James son of Zebedee and his brother John, who were in their boat mending the nets. 20 Immediately he called them; and they left their father Zebedee in the boat with the hired men and followed him.

***

Since arriving in Nashville and beginning my formation as a historical theologian I have undertaken extensive studies of the thought of St.

Augustine, 4th/5th century bishop of the Church in Hippo, in Northern Africa. Prior to these studies I had only the most basic acquaintance with his thinking, my knowledge of his teachings was so limited, in fact, that I was shocked when I stumbled upon the following quote several years ago: *"You called, you cried, you shattered my deafness. You sparkled, you blazed, you drove away my blindness. You shed your fragrance, and I drew in my breath, and I pant for you. I tasted and now I hunger and thirst. You touched me, and now I burn with longing for your peace."*

Lovely words, really. But they caught my attention not because they're lovely, but because of how they contrast with a more familiar quote from Augustine, something those with only minimal awareness of Augustine know, which goes something like this *"Lord, save me. But not yet."* Though Augustine was introduced to Christian faith at an early age, though he nearly accepted baptism at a time of terrible illness as a child, he ultimately resisted giving his heart to Jesus for over three decades. And even after he was baptized at the age of 31, he still struggled to fully give himself over to the call God was extending to him. In order to ordain Augustine to the priesthood he literally had to be chased down by the bishops and he wept as they laid hands on him, feeling unworthy of this calling. So, the passionate devotion suggested by the lovely quote I shared a few moments ago belongs to Augustine's later years and it is markedly different than the quote characterizing his young adulthood *"Oh Lord, save me, but not yet."*

There's not much of this *"not yet"* sentiment evidenced in our scripture readings this morning. In both of our scripture readings this morning we witness immediate conversion. The people of Nineveh hear the cry of a foreign prophet wandering through their massive city and they immediately turn their lives around, evidencing repentance and dependence on God's mercy and forgiveness. We're told the entire city, turns itself around, away from its waywardness and towards God, without hesitation, without delay.

There's no *"not yet"* in this story, it's all about immediate response. And in the Gospel of Matthew a prophet who has just begun his ministry calls out to four men engaged in their daily labor *"Follow me and I will make you fishers of people."* And without hesitation, immediately we're told, Simon and Andrew, James and John, drop everything and follow Jesus.

There's something unnerving about the immediacy of response in both stories, is there not? As we try to imagine ourselves in the sinful city of Nineveh going about our daily business, or on the shores of the Sea of Galilee mending our nets, do we imagine that a one sentence sermon from a strange prophet would immediately compel us to drop everything and follow? Surely not. We'd have goodbyes to say, loose ends to tie up, and arrangements to make to ensure the business of our lives went on—that's if we were even inclined to follow in the first place. We'd surely have suspicions and objections, of the *'Who are you to call me anyways?"* sort. And we may rather like the unhealthy or even death dealing patterns of our daily lives. We know that our bad habits or abusive relationships or addictions aren't any good for us, but we're rather attached to them and at best we're inclined to say *'Um, could you call again later? Save me, Lord, but not yet."* Though one country singer proclaims *'if you're going through hell go quickly so you can get out before the devil even knows you're there,"* when we find ourselves in living hells for some reason, contrary to the advice of this country singer, we often find ourselves inclined to linger, wallow, preferring the devil we know, to the unknown.

Our resistance to immediate and total repentance and discipleship is not really all that new a phenomenon. Not only Saint Augustine in the fourth century, but even the prophet Jonah many centuries before shared this struggle. We pick up the story of Jonah today with his second call from God to bring a message to the people of Nineveh.

And THIS time Jonah decides to listen. Mind you, this is immediately after he's been vomited on the shores of Nineveh by a whale that has swallowed him and held on to him for three days. The FIRST time God called to Jonah, Jonah acted agreeable enough, but had absolutely NO intention of going to that wicked city of Nineveh to which God had called him to go. Nineveh was a city in modern day Iraq. Jonah got on a boat headed for modern day Spain. He went in the exact opposite direction of God's call. A storm blew up and threatened all on the boat that he had chosen to travel on. He allowed the sailors to throw him overboard, sure that his disobedience to God was the source of their troubles and sure enough when Jonah was thrown to the sea, the waters calmed down, a big fish swallowed him up, and there he was left in the belly of that big fish to sit and think and pray for mercy for three days.

Jonah probably thought that this turn of events had made it certain that he wouldn't have to follow-through on God's call, but sure enough, he's vomited up on the shores just outside of Nineveh and hears God call's again. Resigned to this mission, Jonah goes about it. Even after his wildly successful preaching campaign, a campaign which led to the conversion of an entire city, a campaign which thwarted God's original intentions to destroy the city. Jonah is sullen and bitter, wishing God would destroy these wicked foreigners and if he wasn't going to get to see such an exciting show of destruction, he preferred his own death.

Now the book of Jonah was written as a satire intended to teach truths about God and humans, not necessarily literal truth about the experience of an historical figure named Jonah. This book is an excellent example of biblical story that bears truth regardless of its historical veracity. Can we not see ourselves in Jonah? Unwilling to do what God calls us to do. Finding ourselves doing what God has called us to do, but with yet resistant hearts. Unable to grasp and accept the breadth and depth of God's love for us AND for those whom we find it difficult to love. Do we not feel a greater kinship with Jonah than we do with the people of Nineveh, Simon, Andrew, James, and John? Are we not more likely to run, to resist, or to only half-heartedly follow through than to immediately repent or drop everything and follow? Aren't we more likely to make excuses than give in? Do we not often seem to prefer a living death to the true-life God offers?

But deep down, I think, most of us have a yearning to be called and to truly follow. In the people of Nineveh, and in the first four disciples, we see people who are in touch with this yearning enough to indulge it. Some people can turn their lives around and give them to God with seeming immediacy, perhaps because the circumstances of their lives have brought them in touch with this deep yearning. But many holds back, make excuses, wait, ignoring the longing they must be led by Him who brings life and life in all its fullness.

The thing is that God's call is persistent. Even if we fail to respond immediately, God will find a way to reach us, even if it requires something as unpleasant as being vomited by a whale. John Calvin described this as God's irresistible grace. If God is calling you, you can't ultimately keep resisting. Seeing as you're here in church today you may have already given in to the call and are now in the business of following. But then again you may be like Saint Augustine, raised in the church, but not quite sure if you're totally on board, wanting a fuller experience of the saving grace Jesus offers, but just not sure if you're ready for it-yet. Or maybe, you once turned your life around and gave it to Jesus, but recently you've found yourself taking it back and wandering rather than following. Or maybe you're only here because your mother or wife MADE you come, and you are bound and determined to get NOTHING out of this hour. Or maybe your life is spinning out of control and you showed up today hoping to hear something that would make a difference. Whatever the reason you're here today, I know that I'm here today to tell you that Jesus is calling you, calling you to follow him, to let him lead, to let it all go and follow him. You can do so immediately, or you can wait another 15 years. If Jesus is calling though, you're going to respond, so why not today?

Company Kept
Luke 15:1-10 (NRSV)

This sermon was originally written for and delivered to the First Presbyterian Church of Lowville, NY on September 16, 2007.

Luke 15:1-10 (NRSV)

15 Now all the tax collectors and sinners were coming near to listen to him. 2 And the Pharisees and the scribes were grumbling and saying, "This fellow welcome sinner and eats with them."

3 So he told them this parable: 4 "Which one of you, having a hundred sheep and losing one of them, does not leave the ninety-nine in the wilderness and go after the one that is lost until he finds it? 5 When he has found it, he lays it on his shoulders and rejoices. 6 And when he comes home, he calls together his friends and neighbors, saying to them, 'Rejoice with me, for I have found my sheep that was lost.' 7 Just so, I tell you, there will be more joy in heaven over one sinner who repents than over ninety-nine righteous persons who need no repentance.

8 "Or what woman having ten silver coins, if she loses one of them, does not light a lamp, sweep the house, and search carefully until she finds it? 9 When she has found it, she calls together her friends and neighbors, saying, 'Rejoice with me, for I have found the coin that I had lost.' 10 Just so, I tell you, there is joy in the presence of the angels of God over one sinner who repents."

***

I heard a story this week about a young woman and the company she keeps. Now, one could think that I'm implying something negative with this phrase "the company she keeps". We worry so about the associations of our young people, don't we? We worry that they'll fall in with "the wrong crowd", that they'll be tainted by their "so-called friends". I spent some time with someone this week who has two young boys and is already worried, based on some unusual social skills in her brilliant, eldest child, about the friends he is likely to make and the friends he is likely not to make, as he grows. Anyhow, I heard a story this week about a young woman and the company she keeps, specifically the company she kept when she was in high school, particularly during the lunch hour. She tried eating with her peers, those who enjoy learning as much as she does, who share many activities and interests with her, but a certain cattiness seemed prevalent at that lunch table, complaining and judging; she got tired of it, so she sought out new company. She found the best lunch time company at the table with "the druggies". They had fascinating conversations about things that matter, but they exited lunch early most days to engage in behavior in which she was not interested, so she had to find someone to hang with for the rest of the lunch hour. She would make her way to the gym where she'd find "the rejects" and here she found the best company of all. They let her play hacky sack even though she wasn't any good at it. They were kind and happy to have her with them. Now that she is in college, she remembers these lunchtime experiences and seeks out interesting, accepting people for friends-whether most people are interested in or accepting of them.

The day after I heard this story, I opened my Bible to the Gospel reading appointed for this Sunday and it was as if I walked into a high school during lunch hour. At the very beginning of the story we're introduced to different groups-The tax collectors and the sinners (not unlike the rejects and the druggies)-and the Pharisees and the Scribes (the popular kids and the smart ones).

And then there's Jesus. Jesus has just finished a teaching with the words 'Let all who have ears to hear listen." And who is it that is listening to him? It's the tax collectors and the sinners, the rejects and the druggies. The Pharisees and the Scribes, the elite, the smart, popular ones aren't listening. It's hard to listen when your mouth is moving and they're busy grumbling. They may not have been able to learn much from Jesus thanks to their grumbling, but their grumbling helps us to learn something about Jesus. "This fellow welcome sinner and eats with them." One could have gotten the impression that Jesus was standing behind a podium on a stage, or that he was standing on a hilltop, essentially that he was talking down to the little people below, but from the grumblers we learn the picture is not like this at all. Jesus has welcomed these undesirable folks, it's as if he's thrown open the door to his personal home and let them come flooding in to sit down at a table full of food, he has personally prepared. Or to stick with our school lunch image, it's like he went into the gym and gathered up the rejects and invited them and anyone else who was feeling rather lonely to sit and eat with him. And this is a joyful image-you know they're eating pizza-the best the school has to offer. They are content. The popular kids meanwhile aren't managing to savor the pizza, or experience the joy, because they're too busy scowling and grumbling.

Jesus does what Jesus always does when people raise their eyebrows, when they don't seem to understand. He tells a story. He tells three stories. We read just two of them today. The stories Jesus tells though aren't simple morality tales; they're parables. One scholar has defined a parable in this way "at its simplest, the parable is a metaphor or simile drawn from nature or common life, arresting the hearer by its vividness or strangeness, and leaving the mind in sufficient doubt about its precise application to tease it into active thought." Jesus doesn't spoon feed his disciples, he prods, he pokes, he teases, he pushes us to think-to actively think.

The first of the two stories are especially effective towards this goal if we really listen to it. Unfortunately, we may miss a few details because we're so sure we know the story so well. Jesus invites thought initially by framing the story as a question "What man wouldn't do this?" And the "this" he describes is the leaving behind of 99 sheep, that would be 99 percent of his sheep in the wilderness, or the Greek more literally says "in the open", to go after 1 lost sheep. Now apparently there is an old Gospel hymn which seeks to tell this story, but where are the 99 sheep left in that hymn? They are left safely in the fold. But that's not where they are in this story. They're left in the open- where any wolf could get them, where they could wander off. Would most of us do this? Would most of us leave behind 99% of our livelihood in order to reclaim a missing 1%? And if that little detail isn't puzzling enough, how about the fact of throwing a party to which all one's friends and neighbors are invited just because one lost sheep, a sheep who was lost because it had been stupid enough to wander off in the first place, just because one lost sheep had been found? Is Jesus effectively teasing us into active thought?

And that second curiosity, about a party being thrown when the lost is found, is even more curious in the second story-she finds one lost coin and throws a party? The coin was not even an especially valuable coin, necessarily. One is left wondering whether she spent the total of her 10 coins in order to have the party to celebrate the finding of the one. These stories don't seem to be lessons in responsible or even rational economics.

They must have some other truth to teach.

Jesus seems to be suggesting something about the character of God in these stories, that God is in the business of seeking out and finding the lost. There seems to be no question in these stories that the lost will be found, it's simply a question of when and how the lost will be found. This is what God does and God goes to great lengths to do so. And... God doesn't seem to be in the business of seeking out and saving the lost in order to scold them. Once again, we see that God's purpose is to throw a whopping party-maybe even a pizza party.

We're throwing a pizza party in our church basement after the conclusion of our worship and work today-everybody is invited to this pizza party. And later this week we'll have our monthly Stone Soup Kitchen dinner-and everybody is always invited to our Stone Soup Kitchen. We mean it, don't we? We'll make room for anybody who wants to grow in faith through our educational ministries which are being kicked off at our pizza party today and we'll make room for anybody who's hungry at our Stone Soup Kitchen, won't we? Do we? Jesus helps to explain the company he keeps by telling these stories. Jesus leads me to wonder about the company **we** keep through the telling of these stories. We say that all are welcome, but do we, like Jesus, invest our energies in seeking and finding the lost, no matter the cost? Are we truly invested in making sure that everybody, especially the apparent nobody's, can join in the feast? Is everyone able to participate-do they hear the invitation; can they access our facilities? Are we willing keep company with Jesus and with the company he keeps?

Resources in addition to scripture which were cited in the writing of this sermon:

Craddock, Fred B. 1990. *Luke in Interpretation: A Series for Preachers and Teachers.* Louisville, KY: Westminster/John Knox Press.

Dealing with Things as They Are
Acts 17:16-31 (CEB)

This sermon was written for and delivered to St. Andrew's Presbyterian Church in Portland, Oregon on April 29, 2018.

Acts 17:16-31 (CEB)

> 16 While Paul waited for them in Athens, he was deeply distressed to find that the city was flooded with idols. 17 He began to interact with the Jews and Gentile God worshippers in the synagogue. He also addressed whoever happened to be in the marketplace each day. 18 Certain Epicurean and Stoic philosophers engaged him in discussion too. Some said, "What an amateur! What's he trying to say?" Others remarked, "He seems to be a proclaimer of foreign gods." (They said this because he was preaching the good news about Jesus and the resurrection.) 19 They took him into custody and brought him to the council on Mars Hill. "What is this new teaching? Can we learn what you are talking about? 20 You've told us some strange things and we want to know what they mean." (21 They said this because all Athenians as well as the foreigners who live in Athens used to spend their time doing nothing but talking about or listening to the newest thing.)
>
> 22 Paul stood up in the middle of the council on Mars Hill and said, "People of Athens, I see that you are very religious in every way. 23 As I was walking through town and carefully observing your objects of worship, I even found an altar with this inscription: 'To an unknown God.' What you worship as unknown, I now proclaim to you. 24 God, who made the world and everything in it, is Lord of heaven and earth. He doesn't live in temples made with human hands. 25 Nor is God served by human hands, as though he needed something, since he is the one who gives life, breath, and everything else. 26 From one-person God created every human nation to live on the whole earth, having determined their appointed times and the boundaries of their lands. 27 God made the nations so they would seek him, perhaps even reach out to him and find him. In fact, God isn't far away from any of us. 28 In God we live, move, and exist. As some of your own poets said, 'We are his offspring.'
>
> 29 "Therefore, as God's offspring, we have no need to imagine that the divine being is like a gold, silver, or stone image made by human skill

and thought. 30 God overlooks ignorance of these things in times past, but now directs everyone everywhere to change their hearts and lives. 31 This is because God has set a day when he intends to judge the world justly by a man he has appointed. God has given proof of this to everyone by raising him from the dead."

***

I've been working on developing a meditation practice the past several months. I started with just five minutes of sitting, centered breathing, but I'm up to 15 now. Some days less, but occasionally I do manage to be still for a full 15 minutes now. I have a friend who is coaching me through this practice, and he recommended early on that I focus my mind on a simple mantra—he suggested the mantra "Look for the good." That worked well for a while.

One morning last week I was scrolling through e-mail while half awake (trying to break this habit, by the way) and I opened an e-mail I usually delete without reading. I don't know why I opened it. And I read it. And in that e-mail, I found a mantra that I truly need— "I will deal with things as they are, *not* as I think they SHOULD be." What does this mean? To me it's related to the idea that expectations are premeditated resentments. When I operate out of expectations, I'm often going to be disappointed. And resentment quickly follows. And resentment is poison. It's also about suspending judgment. And dealing with what's before me, honoring it for what it is, working with reality not fantasy. I know I'm dealing with things as I think they SHOULD be when I'm experiencing all sorts of interior discomfort and distress. Sometimes dealing with things as they are is painful, for sure, but it's different than the irritation or discomfort that comes from dealing with things as I think they should be.

So, I've been sitting with this mantra for about a week now, so it was no surprise when I ended up seeing this week's story about Paul as a perfect illustration of its wisdom. Last week I was a bit hard on Paul as I unpacked his missed opportunity, and one might even say irresponsibility, in relationship to the slave woman. I acknowledged that he, like us, remained human after his baptism. And that he, like us, has better and worse days in his ministry as a witness to the resurrected Christ. Today, I think, we're seeing a better day, and I think it's better because Paul is managing to deal with Athens as it is, not as he thinks it should be. But I'll get back to that.

First, when last we left Paul he was with Silas in Philippi. Remember, they had just been released from prison. Now he's alone in Athens waiting for them... hunh? Well, a bit of time and travel has elapsed since last we were together. From Philippi, Paul and Silas went on to Thessalonica. They were initially very positively received in the synagogues there, but they ended up the targets of some intense hostility. They moved on from there to Beroea—things got off to an even better start there, but then the hostile troublemakers from Thessalonica followed them there and stirred up controversy. The believers in Beroea wanted to distance Paul from the trouble so they secreted him away, as far away as they could get him—all the way to Athens, the ancient capital of Greece, the capital of the then Roman province of Achaia. He left Silas and Timothy behind and was waiting for them to catch up to him. So now we're caught up.

So, Paul is on his own in this great, historical city, but is he awestruck by the monuments all about? No. He is greatly distressed. Everywhere he looks he sees idols—human creations that are worshipped as gods. The Book of Acts tells us the city was flooded with idols. Now, Paul as a faithful Jew, had a deep aversion to idolatry. What is the number one commandment? Thou shalt have no other gods before me.... And the second? Thou shalt make no graven image. He has definite ideas about how things SHOULD be. And this stirs up that interior distress and discomfort of which I spoke before.

We know that Paul has a temper. We saw it last week. Read the letter to the Galatians if you're not sure about this. He could have gone on a rant, shaming and scolding the Athenians for their idolatry. It's not hard to imagine Paul doing this. Anne Lamott says this about Paul in her book *Hallelujah Anyway*, 'Putting aside the little problem with all the people he had killed, he was annoying, sexist, stuffy, and theoretical... He often got preachy, and his message was frequently about trying to be more stoic, with dogmatic 'Shape up' and 'Shame on you' talks. He was cranky, judgmental, and self-righteous, worse even than I.' She has more to say about him, some of it even good. But all these things may well be true about Paul... and I think they may be reflective of moments when he was dealing with people, the church, the world as he thought they SHOULD be rather than as they were.

But somehow, in Athens, he managed to be different. He acknowledged that he was in a radically different context. Toto, I don't think we're in Jerusalem anymore... And he just tried to take it all in, as it was—how do I know that this is what he did? Well, he noticed an inscription on an altar 'to an unknown God.' You must get close to absorb inscriptions, usually. Often, I don't take the time to read the small plaques on public statues or the words carved in the stone. He kept his eyes wide open.

I also notice that he started out in the synagogues, in the company of those who shared his foundational faith commitments, those who might be as averse to idolatry, those with whom he had plenty of starting points for conversation. Likely in the synagogues he opened the scriptures and shared his understanding of how Jesus fulfills the promises of the Hebrew Bible. This is what we see him doing in the synagogues in Thessalonica and Beroea earlier in the section. The translation from which I read today said that he was **interacting** with those he found in the synagogues, but he was **addressing** whomever he found in the marketplace. The difference in verbs suggest it was more possible to have dialogue and conversation in the synagogues. There was less of a cultural gap. I think this choice to begin in the synagogues was also a good way of dealing with things as they were... a good way to realize there was more to reality in Athens than the pagan idolatry that first offended him and draw strength from conversations that came more naturally to him.

But he also spent time in the marketplace. The marketplace was the center of life in Athens; it "was the main public square and center of Greek cultural life. It was surrounded by open porches and columns, which served as gathering places for philosophical discussion and debate."It seems it was not uncommon for men to pontificate in the marketplace, so Paul joined in. Our translation says he was judged an amateur. Other translations say he was considered a babbler. A literal translation suggests he was a "seed picker" which is a slam on inexperienced teachers who pick up odd bits of information here and there and spit them out without thinking. Some think he's proclaiming foreign gods... Jesus being one, and resurrection another— the concept of resurrection, was so foreign, some may have thought it was a name, Anastasis. In any case, in the marketplace the cultural gap is huge, and there is a failure to communicate.

I'm guessing though that he wasn't leading with judgment and shame... because when he is taken to the Aeropagus, before the council, those who take him there make it plain that they simply wish to understand him. They want to know if they even can understand him. It is curiosity rather than anger or fear that opens this hearing. I think Paul had to be speaking in a gentle and generous way to nurture such curiosity.

Again, dealing with things as they are, not as he thought they should be. And then the speech in the Aeropagus... he begins by praising or flattering the Athenians, praising them for the very thing that first offended him so deeply. He demonstrates an acceptance of things as they are when he praises them for their deep religiosity, evidenced by their many objects of worship. It is always easier to get someone to listen to you if you begin by validating your listener in some way. It's a good rhetorical move. Shaming them for their idolatry would have grown out of his feelings about how things should be, praise for religiosity emerged from dealing with things as they were.

And... it's more than just rhetoric. He is finding a point of connection, a bridge across the cultural gap... I'm religious. You're religious. I worship. You worship. He then lifts a cultural artifact of their own—that inscription on an altar to *"An unknown God."* Now, this might have been intended to cover their bases... there were altars and monuments to all sorts of gods all over the city, the hill on which the Aeropagus sat was dedicated to Mars, the god of war... this altar left open the possibility that there was a god they had not yet met. Paul took it as an opportunity to proclaim the God he knows, and has come to know better through Jesus Christ, the God above all gods. But he is starting with something of theirs... with something he found among them...

And he doesn't say much at all about Jesus. He focuses on the creator God, the source of all that is. He is trying open reflection on the pointlessness of worshipping idols, by evoking an understanding of the God in whom we all live, and move, and have our being... That's another quote, by the way, from a Greek poet, so is the *"We are his offspring"*—he's using their literature, speaking their language... seeking to open new insights, by dealing with things as they are now. This offspring language got me thinking about water... It's as if the creator God is the ocean, and we're rivers and streams flowing away from the ocean, and our creations, the works of our hands and minds, are the creeks forking off from us. Our worship, our praise, our thanksgiving ought to be directed to our source... that vast life force on which we absolutely depend, not on the many things we create.

At the very end of his speech he delivers the most common preaching message throughout the book of Acts—change your hearts and lives—older translations simply say—repent—and he suggests that one man, a vague reference to Jesus, has been appointed as judge and that he has been authorized as judge of the living and the dead by God's choice to resurrect him from the dead. This is a very different message than that which he typically preaches. He doesn't tell the story of Jesus' life and death, he only vaguely references his resurrection and anticipated return. He doesn't quote any scriptures. He does his best to honor things as they are... so that maybe some will be able to hear him, and enter conversation with him, and perhaps even come to faith in Jesus through his witness.

We didn't read the end of the chapter. It turns out he had a mixed reception. Some believed. Some scoffed. And so, it always is. But... from the marketplace where he was mocked as a seed picker and misunderstood as a proclaimer of foreign divinities... to a situation where some could hear and understand and accept what he was saying... this is massive progress. And with the benefit of history we know that Christianity really did take root in Greece, and Paul played a major role in scattering the seeds that eventually grew.

I think this insight that we need to deal with things as they are, not as we think they should be is useful on a lot of levels, in many aspects of our lives. But for right now I want us to think about what it teaches us about our ministry of Christian witness. We are in a city where many would claim that they are spiritual but not religious, where all manner of new age spiritualities thrive, where there is distrust of institutions, and certainly of the church. And yet we are in a city where a yearning for the holy is on display in myriad ways. If we want to be witnesses to the resurrected Christ here in Portland, we need to find ways to honor our neighbors as they are, to meet them where they are, and to find points of connection, bridges between us and them. We may wish that our church were bursting at the seams with people and that all the churches were... that it were as hard to find a seat in pews as it is to find a seat in a coffeehouse or pub... but we need to get ourselves to the coffeehouses and pubs, to the yoga studios and tattoo parlors, to the dog parks and rallies... to listen deeply to the people we meet there, to observe carefully, and eventually to speak cautiously of the love we've found that will not let us go, the satisfaction to the yearning that is on display all around us all the time, the God revealed in Jesus. Not everyone will be able to hear and accept what we have to share. But some might. And we can rest well at night knowing that we are honoring our call as disciples of Jesus to witness even to the ends of the earth.

Resources in addition to scripture that influenced or were cited in this sermon:

I managed to delete the e-mail in which I found the mantra, but it came through a meditation app called *Breethe*. https://breethe.com/

Anne Lamott, *Hallelujah Anyway*, New York: Riverhead Books, 2017.

I derived a lot from the notes in my *Common English Study Bible* this week. This is an excellent resource for scriptural study.

YES!!!!!!
Psalm 19 (NRSV)

This sermon was originally written for and delivered to the First Presbyterian Church of Lowville, NY in a Lenten series on Prayer, on March 19, 2006.

Psalm 19 (NRSV)

1 The heavens are telling the glory of God; and the firmament proclaims his handiwork.

2 Day to day pours forth speech, and night to night declares knowledge. 3 There is no speech, nor are there words; their voice is not heard;

4 yet their voice goes out through all the earth, and their words to the end of the world. In the heavens he has set a tent for the sun, which comes out like a bridegroom from his wedding canopy, and like a strong man runs its course with joy. 6 Its rising is from the end of the heavens, and its circuit to the end of them; and nothing is hid from its heat.

7 The law of the Lord is perfect, reviving the soul; the decrees of the Lord are sure, making wise the simple; 8 the precepts of the Lord are right, rejoicing the heart; the commandment of the Lord is clear, enlightening the eyes; 9 the fear of the Lord is pure, enduring forever; the ordinances of the Lord are true and righteous altogether. More to be desired are they then gold, even much fine gold; sweeter also than honey, and drippings of the honeycomb.

10 Moreover, by them is your servant warned; in keeping them there is great reward. But who can detect their errors? Clear me from hidden faults.

11 Keep back your servant also from the insolent; [d]do not let them have dominion over me. Then I shall be blameless, and innocent of great transgression.

12 Let the words of my mouth and the meditation of my heart be acceptable to you, O Lord, my rock and my redeemer.

***

Often when people tell me they don't know how to pray, or that they are afraid to pray, or that they are sure they don't pray right, I share with them Annie Lamott's accounting of the two best prayers she knows "Thank you. Thank you. Thank you." and "Help me. Help me. Help me." And most of the time I see their faces and shoulders relax, because everyone and anyone can and does pray these two prayers. Thanks to Annie Lamott I'm able to send the worried Christian away a little less worried, and a little more aware of how easy it is to be connected to God in prayer.

This week I realized that there's another simple, and fabulous prayer, that could be added to Annie's short list to the same effect. I call this the "YES!" prayer. This is a prayer we pray as naturally as the "Thank you. Thank you. Thank you's" that follow the experience of blessings, and as naturally as the "Help me. Help me. Help ME's" that bubble up in a crisis. This is a prayer that sings in us at moments when all seems right with the world.

Sometimes really good food makes us pray it. There was a dish I would make in seminary that had potatoes and cabbage and sour cream and other creamy goodness and savory seasoning and whenever I would make it my seminary roommate would say "Everything that's right in the world is in this dish." More simply put "YES!" Sometimes breathtaking views of creation makes us pray it. I remember coming around the bend on my way into the Canadian Rockies and catching a glimpse of snow peaked mountain tops for the first time ever and feeling the breath sucked out of me by my awe at their grandeur "YES!" Sometimes rites of passage make us pray it. I remember walking to the dining hall at Vanderkamp, the space in which I did not want to be married, but the space in which the rain required us to be married. We took a detour through the reception tent and I saw the tables beautifully set and the cake so beautifully decorated, and then when we arrived at the dining hall I saw SO MANY people that I love and Kevin loves and that love us, and I saw Kevin, my love, and a smile took possession of my face that did not leave me for the next four hours. Everything was just right, "YES!"

Have you noticed that as we age these "YES!" moments, these moments when our souls sing, when we tremble with awe, when we are certain of God's goodness and glory, have you noticed that these moments seem to come fewer and farther between? Children, especially young children seem to be able to pray this prayer daily. I think of the young girl who captured my heart this past week when she made a bee line to my parent's dining room table ready for chocolate cake. Her anticipation of that cake, her enjoyment of the cake, her intense focus on the cake... all of it seemed to embody a "YES!" As did her delight in the rub on tattoo she got at the Dinosaur Barbeque the next day, and then insisted everyone at the table get one too. Most little kids seem to be able to find a *"YES!"* in most every day.

One of my favorite songs is a song written and performed by Christine Lavin called *"Katy says today is the best day of my whole entire life"*. I'd like to share that song with you now.

*Katy says, "today is the best day
of my whole entire life."
Katy is three years old.
We've been dancing in the living room
to her new Tom Paxton record.
Katy's got a lot of rhythm when she wiggles
for a little kid, she's got soul.
That night when her mom and dad get home,
I tell them what she said to me,
figure they'll think I'm babysitting genius to make their little girl so
darn happy.
But they smile and they say
"Now don't take this the wrong way.
But Katy said the same thing yesterday.
Lately she's been saying that every day."
I think back to what I know
was the best day of my life.
It was winter time ten years ago.
We were staying in a farmhouse
in the middle of Vermont.
The hills were covered with Christmas trees
and freshly fallen snow.
Instantly I picture the vivid details of that day
when you told me that you loved me more than you could ever say.
The air was a bracing cold;
the sky a startled blue.
Never or since have I felt that close to you.
What does that say about you and me
and the past ten years?
I've learned to live with your silence,
you've learned to overlook my tears.
Now this dancing three-year-old
in her simple, perfect way
has me questioning the basis
for this life we live today.
Katy's probably sleeping now.*

*I wonder if she dreams
about flying with the angels,
dancing with moon beams.
You are here beside me.
You are snoring right out loud.
I long to kiss you on the forehead
and smooth your worried brow.
Though we have not given up,
it's been ages since we've tried
to reveal the aching passion
that for years we've pushed aside.
I whisper that "I love you."
because I know you cannot hear.
I turn off the light and in the dark
you gently pull me near.
Katy says "today is the best day
of my whole entire life."*

In this simple, perfect song we see the freedom with which children pray prayers of praise and adoration, "YES!" prayers, and the struggle it can be for adults. It's not that we've given up, but it's been ages since many of us have tried. Ages since we've tried to tune into the wonder of this world on any regular basis. Ages since we've tried to reveal the aching passion that the glories of God's creation and the gifts of our relationships and the goodness of life stirs in us. My friend Theresa who's a pastor in Ohio says that she has no problem praying prayers of thanksgiving, prayers of intercession and petition, prayers of confession, but prayers of praise and adoration are hard. It's hard to bring that feeling of awe and wonder to the surface on command, to muster up a "YES!" out of nothing.

The Psalmist would remind us that at every moment there is reason for our souls to sing out a "YES!" For we need only gaze at the stars, see the sun running its course, to be reminded of God's glory and stirred to praise "YES!" We need only contemplate the gift of God's teaching to us, God's willingness to show us how to live, to lay out a path for us to follow, to guide us into what is right, to be stirred to praise and adoration, for this is like honey, the psalmist says, sweet honey dripping from the honeycomb, "YES!" It's not that life gets less wonder-full as we age, we get less wonder-aware as we age, at least some of us, many of us do. But we can try, try to pause and invite wonder and praise to course through our veins again.

This past Thursday, I asked the residents at the East Road Adult Home to think back to "YES!" moments in their lives and one of the men said, 'Some of them are happy and some of them are sad." I asked him to share what he was thinking of and he said "Well, I'm thinking of when my wife was ill for so long and when she finally died. That was one of those moments." "YES! God is good." I replied. He smiled. I asked the residents if any of them had children. One of the women said "Lady, I had 12 children, but I lost one of them." She began to cry. I asked her if she could remember the births of those 12 children. "Kind of" she said. I said, "Can you remember holding each of those 12 babies for the first time?" She sighed and smiled broadly, and I knew we had found what we were looking for. "YES! God is good."

What comes to mind for you? What moments have led to such a "YES!" for you? Remembering these moments can help us tune into the "YES!" moments happening all the time, every day. Katy says, "Today is the best day of my whole entire life." May we say so too. YES! This is prayer. Amen.

Works Cited in this Sermon:

Anne Lamott. *Traveling Mercies*. New York: Pantheon Books, 1999.

Christine Lavin. "Katy Says Today is the Best Day in my Whole Entire Life", on her album *Compass*, released 1991 by Philo.

Section Four

Being the Church

Chesed
Ruth 4 (CEB)

This sermon was written for and delivered to St. Andrew's Presbyterian Church in Portland, Oregon on August 19, 2018, concluding a summer Narrative Lectionary Series (year 4) on the book of Ruth.

Ruth (CEB)

> *4 Meanwhile, Boaz went up to the gate and sat down there. Just then, the redeemer about whom Boaz had spoken was passing by. He said, "Sir, come over here and sit down." So, he turned aside and sat down. 2 Then he took ten men from the town's elders and said, "Sit down here." And they sat down.*
>
> *3 Boaz said to the redeemer, "Naomi, who has returned from the field of Moab, is selling the portion of the field that belonged to our brother Elimelech. 4 I thought that I should let you know and say, 'Buy it, in the presence of those sitting here and in the presence of the elders of my people.' If you will redeem it, redeem it; but if you won't redeem it, tell me so that I may know. There isn't anyone to redeem it except you, and I'm next in line after you."*
>
> *He replied, "I will redeem it."*
>
> *5 Then Boaz said, "On the day when you buy the field from Naomi, you also buy Ruth the Moabite, the wife of the dead man, in order to preserve the dead man's name for his inheritance."*
>
> *6 But the redeemer replied, "Then I can't redeem it for myself, without risking damage to my own inheritance. Redeem it for yourself. You can have my right of redemption, because I'm unable to act as redeemer."*
>
> *7 In Israel, in former times, this was the practice regarding redemption and exchange to confirm any such matter: a man would take off his sandal and give it to the other person. This was the process of making a transaction binding in Israel. 8 Then the redeemer said to Boaz, "Buy it for yourself," and he took off his sandal.*
>
> *9 Boaz announced to the elders and all the people, "Today you are witnesses that I've bought from the hand of Naomi all that belonged to Elimelech and all that belonged to Chilion and Mahlon. 10 And also*

Ruth the Moabite, the wife of Mahlon, I've bought to be my wife, to preserve the dead man's name for his inheritance so that the name of the dead man might not be cut off from his brothers or from the gate of his hometown—today you are witnesses."

11 Then all the people who were at the gate and the elders said, "We are witnesses. May the Lord grant that the woman who is coming into your household be like Rachel and like Leah, both of whom built up the house of Israel. May you be fertile in Ephrathah and may you preserve a name in Bethlehem. 12 And may your household be like the household of Perez, whom Tamar bore to Judah—through the children that the Lord will give you from this young woman."

13 So Boaz took Ruth, and she became his wife.

He was intimate with her, the Lord let her become pregnant, and she gave birth to a son. 14 The women said to Naomi, "May the Lord be blessed, who today hasn't left you without a redeemer. May his name be proclaimed in Israel. 15 He will restore your life and sustain you in your old age. Your daughter-in-law who loves you has given birth to him. She's better for you than seven sons." 16 Naomi took the child and held him to her breast, and she became his guardian. 17 The neighborhood women gave him a name, saying, "A son has been born to Naomi." They called his name Obed. He became Jesse's father and David's grandfather.

18 These are the generations of Perez: Perez became the father of Hezron, 19 Hezron the father of Ram, Ram the father of Amminadab, 20 Amminadab the father of Nahshon, Nahshon the father of Salmon, 21 Salmon the father of Boaz, Boaz the father of Obed, 22 Obed the father of Jesse, and Jesse the father of David.

***

And so, we come to the end to the short book of Ruth. I heard through the grapevine that at least one of you read this little book from start to end and found it rather uninspiring. I doubt that you found Pastor Yolanda or Dr. Jennifer's interpretations of it similarly uninspiring, but on its surface the Book of Ruth does seem a rather ordinary story of ordinary people dealing with life's hardships, deploying cultural practices that seem a bit odd to us. There's not even much mention of God in the story.

Well... perhaps there's something to the mundane character of this story... aren't we too ordinary people living ordinary lives in a world that, on its surface, doesn't have much to say about God? Aren't we dealing with life's hardships deploying cultural practices that make a world of sense right now, but will seem strange in a couple hundred years... maybe even in a couple decades?

This last chapter is, I think, particularly hard to wrap our minds around. Scholars say the opening scene is humorous, but I think that humor is lost on us. [I didn't hear much chuckling as we read it.] There was someone in Naomi's family who was closer kin to Naomi and her dead husband Elimelech than Boaz. So, according to the customs of the day he needed to be given the opportunity to redeem all that belonged to Elimelech, in order to keep it in the family. This meant purchasing property, and the women that attach to this property. This is offensive to our modern ears. Naomi and Ruth are property to be negotiated over in the town square. The other possible redeemer is never named. He's interested in gaining some land, but not interested in caring for widows and possibly children. Maybe it's because he doesn't want a foreign wife. Boaz emphasizes Ruth's outsider status. Maybe it's because he can't afford the care of a larger family. We don't know. He won't preserve Elimelech's name, so he's not even given a name. Boaz, it seems, has developed great affection for Ruth and wants to marry her. He is more interested in taking care of this family than in possessing their land. His name is remembered.

Ruth's name is remembered too, obviously, a book is named after her. But what I find interesting is the way that she disappears in this last chapter. After being taken in marriage to Boaz she is never named again. The child she births is given to Naomi to nurse. I noted several scholars declaring this a miracle of God, an older woman becoming a wet nurse by God's providence. But I'm left wondering about Ruth's engorged breasts. And what grief accompanied handing over her son. And I'm left wondering why Naomi so rarely expresses appreciation to or care for Ruth. Ruth bravely acts to restore Naomi's status and fortune at great risk to herself and by the end of the story she's invisible.

This reminds me of a song I heard a woman sing this summer, a song she wrote about her mother. She could barely sing it for all the emotion it stirred in her. The refrain of this song is 'She's always been somebody's something. She's been everything but alone. A daughter, a lover, a wife, and a mother— She's lived every life but her own.*"*

The genealogy at the end of our chapter leaves out Ruth's name, as was typical for the time, the line is traced through fathers... The son she bore is linked to his father Boaz who was descended from Perez and was a descendent of King David. The most celebrated, if complicated, king in Israel's history. This ordinary person, a foreign widow, a migrant fleeing famine, births a child who continues the line that produces Israel's greatest king.

I listened to three scholars discussing the Book of Ruth on a podcast this week. They noted that all the summer series of the Narrative Lectionary have focused us on love of neighbor. At their heart, the ten commandments teach us to love our neighbors, give us boundaries for ordering love of neighbors. And the 1st Letter of John focuses heavily on love of neighbor, as the sermon from Cynthia Reynolds made so plain. And the Book of Ruth is a story that depicts love of neighbor.

I have been suggesting some ways that our modern or post-modern ears might find the story falling short in loving Ruth, but to conclude this morning I want draw our attention to the love that does come through in this simple story. And I want us to learn from this and from the failings in the story to better love our neighbors.

A powerful Hebrew word is repeated throughout this short book. That word is *Chesed* which means steadfast love or lovingkindness. It's a hard word to translate.

Here's what one scholar has to say about *"Chesed"*:

"It's one of the Bible's most important concepts. *Chesed* חֶסֶד should be a word on your lips, whether you know Hebrew or not. For Jews it should be as easy as saying Shabbat or shalom. For Christians it should be as easy as saying agape or ekklesia. It is used 297 times in the Bible."

This scholar goes on to say 'Ruth is a book about *Chesed*, a chain of acts of kindness, that transform the lives of some people living in a dark time (the days of the Judges). This chain of *Chesed* leads to something more extraordinary than anyone could have imagined. The lives of a few obscure people in Israel's agrarian past become seeds of Messianic hope on the earth."

You can use the link in my sermon manuscript to read a list of demonstrations of *Chesed* that abound in this short book and more about *Chesed* in the Hebrew Bible as a whole. I think that Pastor Yolanda and Dr. Jennifer have already highlighted a few. Ruth certainly demonstrates *Chesed* towards Naomi. Boaz towards Ruth and Naomi. But did you notice the crowds of people in this last chapter? I think there's some *Chesed* there too. Boaz gathers around him witnesses to the transaction he intends to undertake with the unnamed closer kinsmen. After the deal is made, the witnesses speak words of blessing over Boaz and Ruth, wishing them fertility, stitching them into Israel's story... even though Ruth is a foreigner, a member of a foreign group excluded from temple worship according to Deuteronomy.

And then after the baby is born, but before he is transferred to Naomi's breast, a crowd of women gather round her and speak... seeking to lift her out of the despair that had led her to change her name to Mara, meaning bitterness. The speak to her of God's faithfulness. And of Ruth's faithfulness to Naomi, an embodiment of God's faithfulness for her. **They don't name Ruth, but they see her. And they honor her. They speak words that are shocking in that cultural context—** *'She's better for you than seven sons."* Remember, women are property. Of little value, but they ascribe great value to her. Earlier in the book when Naomi mourns her emptiness, it seems she can't see she has not lost *everything*. She yet has Ruth. At the end of the story the women try to help her see this truth. She has not lost everything. She yet has Ruth, and now the beautiful new life born from Ruth's womb.

I'm delighted by the role of the community as witnesses, as extenders of blessing, and as reminders of God's faithful love. I'm delighted by the role of the community welcoming Ruth, a vulnerable and marginal one they easily could have rejected, into their fold. I see *Chesed* in this community. *Chesed* manifested in love of neighbor.

And friends, I see *Chesed* in *this* community, the ordinary fellowship that gathers at the corner of Sunset and Dosch. I see it in the ways you consistently embody your mission to serve your neighbors, demonstrating lovingkindness in ways small and large, loving your neighbor through service all the time. And I see it in the ways you so faithfully love and serve one another—at another funeral reception yesterday, at the start of worship today, via FaceBook encouragement to a young mom who recently broke a bone in her foot. And so, I am delighted that you fine people who feed so many in so many ways will be fed today. Who doesn't love waffles? So, let yourself taste the sweet *Chesed* of God by staying for the party after church. Let yourself be cared for that you might be renewed for ever more faithful service in the year ahead. We hope you know how much we value you. And we hope that all of us will grow in our ability to value every child of God whom we encounter.

Works cited in or that influenced this sermon:

http://www.thehebrewnerd.com/introduction-to-ruth-as-a-book-of-*Chesed*/ (This is where you can learn more about the concept of *Chesed* and how it appears in Ruth.)

http://www.workingpreacher.org/narrative_podcast.aspx?podcast_id=1033, This podcast discusses the whole book of Ruth, if you're interested in hearing other perspectives. It influenced some dimension

For full lyrics to the Kaci Bolls' song, see https://www.musixmatch.com/lyrics/Kaci-Bolls/Somebody-s-Something, I was introduced to this song through Malcolm Gladwell's Podcast, Revisionist History, episode 30, Analysis, Parapraxis, and Elvis, http://revisionisthistory.com/episodes/30-analysis-parapraxis-elvis. You can listen to a recording of the song via this link, https://youtu.be/TqT8JgK8eE4

It's Not About Me.
1 Corinthians 1:10-18 (NRSV)

This sermon was prepared for and delivered to the First Presbyterian Church of Elkhart, Indiana in April of 2015, six months into my co-pastorate there. C Cubed is short for "Curious Christians Connecting," a small group Bible Study I designed to bring together worshippers from different worship services in learning and fellowship.

1 Corinthians 1:10-18 (NRSV)

> 10 Now I appeal to you, brothers and sisters, by the name of our Lord Jesus Christ, that all of you agree and that there be no divisions among you, but that you be united in the same mind and the same purpose. 11 For it has been reported to me by Chloe's people that there are quarrels among you, my brothers and sisters. 12 What I mean is that each of you says, "I belong to Paul," or "I belong to Apollos," or "I belong to Cephas," or "I belong to Christ." 13 Has Christ been divided? Was Paul crucified for you? Or were you baptized in the name of Paul? 14 I thank God that I baptized none of you except Crispus and Gaius, 15 so that no one can say that you were baptized in my name. 16 (I did baptize also the household of Stephanas; beyond that, I do not know whether I baptized anyone else.) 17 For Christ did not send me to baptize but to proclaim the gospel, and not with eloquent wisdom, so that the cross of Christ might not be emptied of its power.
>
> 18 For the message about the cross is foolishness to those who are perishing, but to us who are being saved it is the power of God.

***

I'm finding it fascinating that the last time I preached on this passage for a congregation, I had been preaching for that congregation for a bit more than six months. And so, it is now. This has been, and will continue to be, through the next few hours, a week of reflecting on the first six months of shared ministry of first ever co-pastors here at the First Presbyterian Church of Elkhart. Pastor Rebecca and I are marking this milestone by sharing worship leadership today and by sitting down with whomever would like to join us to offer feedback on our shared ministry at 10:00 a.m. in the reception room and at noon in the fellowship hall. We do hope you'll come.

Looking back, the weeks leading up to the start of our ministry were bumpy, were they not? Grief, anxiety, disagreement were all running high in this congregation. It was particularly hard for some to say goodbye to Pastor David. Just as it had been hard for some to say goodbye to Pastor Nan. And to Pastors Steve and Kathleen before them.

And I could go back and name many more names, couldn't I? In 175 years of Presbyterian ministry in Elkhart a lot of pastors have come and gone. And every transition has brought challenge as well as blessing. Fair enough?

Well, I'm happy to say though challenge has not disappeared, there have been many blessings among us in these 6 months. I take no credit for these blessings; I'm sure that Pastor Rebecca doesn't take credit either. All blessings are gifts from God. But we do rejoice in strong participation in the Discovering our Strengths initiative and the vision that emerged from that process that will guide the work of our leadership. We rejoice in growth in adult education participation. We rejoice in the continuation of the strong ministry of music and children's ministry in this place. We rejoice in the vibrant worship unfolding in three spaces in this church building—and the powerful times when we have combined worshipping congregations for joint worship. We rejoice in the generosity of this congregation—blessing those in need in our community at large and helping to sustain our ministries. We rejoice in the incredible care this community provides to one another. There are many signs of life and faithfulness in this church.

Thanks be to God.

But let's be honest, through the transition, there was loss. People left. It is hard for me to assess the impact of this as most left before we began our ministry here, but I have been in churches all my life. I know how much it hurts when people leave. I know how awkward it is when you bump into someone who has left. I know how hard it is when there is negative chatter about your church in the wider community. I know how much we can miss people and how much, sometimes, we feel resentment or anger towards those who have walked away. A mixed swirl of emotion accompanies church division. I know. Deeply, I know.

So, did members and leaders of the early church. It is no accident that this second round of C cubed is focusing on the first letter to the Corinthians and that we've opted to preach on passages from this letter this month and next. As I suggested to those gathered on Wednesday evening, this book of the Bible captures a living moment of communication to a living church with problems. It thus often speaks fresh to living churches today... with problems of our own.

Many suggest that verse ten of this first chapter, the first verse we read today, represents the thesis, or the main argument, of this entire letter to the Corinthians. "Now I appeal to you, brothers and sisters, by the name of our Lord Jesus Christ, that all of you should be in agreement and that there should be no divisions among you, but that you should be united in the same mind and the same purpose." With this plea to the church in Corinth I hear the voice of a concerned parent... this is the way things SHOULD be, children, no divisions, united in the same mind and the same purpose... the use of the word "should" indicates that this is not, in fact, the way things are. If an appeal is being made, there is work that needs to be done to arrive at these goals. And this entire letter is trying to make the importance of this work and the nature of this work totally clear.

Though many suggest that the conflict here, in Elkhart, in this congregation, has died down dramatically the past several months, someone just said to me the other day "Things are so much calmer now." I think we could all readily agree that being united in the same mind and purpose is yet a vision to be fulfilled here. It is for us, a mature church of 175 years, as it was for the very new church in Corinth, a work in progress.

The interesting thing, though, is that it appears that the Corinthian church didn't think they had a problem with unity. Chapter seven suggests that they wrote a letter to Paul enumerating the problems they were having for which they desired input from their founding apostle, but for the first six chapters of this letter Paul doesn't take up their presenting concerns. Instead, he beats a drum for unity. The main argument of the letter to which he returns again and again all throughout the letter is the appeal to unity stated at the start of our passage today. They think they've got problems with sexual immorality, meat eating, etc. He thinks, based on reports he's receiving about them, that their root problem is division.

What he's hearing is that there are quarrels among them, that they seem to be breaking up into factions claiming loyalty to different teachers and preachers. Some were in Paul's camp. Some in the camp of Apollos (likely a far more eloquent speaker than Paul.) And some in the camp of Cephas-this is probably a reference to Peter who may or may not have ever visited the community himself. But some, apparently, were claiming allegiance to Christ. This would seem to be a good thing, based on everything else Paul has to say, but... if this claim was made to put some in a position of relative superiority over the others, we begin to see the problem. "You belong to Paul? Well, I belong to Christ." The Corinthian community is fragmenting, note the repeated use of the pronoun "I" and the use of the word each... **each** of you is saying I... I... I... Though their baptisms render them one in Christ Jesus, they are splitting into many. And it seems likely that some were claiming to be better than others.

Though there was officially only one congregation in Corinth at the time this letter was written, this congregation was subdivided into several house churches, mirroring the general organization of the city into distinct households. It isn't hard to imagine that a growing congregation that meets in several distinct sub-groupings on a regular basis might be ripe for quarrels and divisions. You know best the people with whom you eat on a regular basis and those with whom you fellowship and study. You trust best the people you know. And distrust of those you don't know is common.

So, let's focus the microscope on First Presbyterian Elkhart, shall we? We have three worship services (I am NOT suggesting we change this, all our services are gifts to us, I'm just making a note), how well do people know each other across the services? I regularly hear church members say that they don't recognize or know people who are regular, faithful worshippers in one of the services of this congregation. Again, not knowing one another can quickly lead to distrust and division. Perhaps things are calmer now, but I want you to closely consider what work you might need to do for the greater health and unity of your congregation. Wednesday night suppers and C cubed seems to be helping a great deal. And Sunday School Classes, Choir, Bible Studies, etc. all can be GREAT opportunities for spiritual growth and deepening relationships with brothers and sisters in Christ, BUT they can also be opportunities for divisions. Small groups in the church *can*, like house churches *can*, though don't necessarily need to, lead to fragmentation and distrust among different subgroups.

We all have comfort zones in church. Perhaps yours in the choir loft, or maybe it is the youth group. Maybe it's even the board of elders, deacons, or Trustees. But how are you cultivating relationships *outside* your comfort zones in this congregation? How might you do this in the months ahead? Where do you sit at fellowship meals? With your immediate family or oldest and dearest friends? Might you find a different dining companion at each meal you attend? Where and with whom do you sit in worship? With your family and maybe your dearest friend from Sunday School? Might you move about week to week, making a point to learn a name that you haven't learned yet or find out how you might be in prayer for a brother and sister you barely know? If division has happened before in this congregation, it can happen again. But it doesn't have to happen. The appeal of this passage, brothers and sisters, is for us.

One clear word of caution that we can take from this passage of scripture is the danger that rests in over identifying with human leaders. What matters, Paul insists, is not the person who is preaching, but the message that is being preached. In the appeal at the start of this passage Paul names everyone in the community a brother or sister and speaks of **our** Lord Jesus Christ. The Lordship of Jesus Christ is the basis for the unity of the community. No particularly charismatic leader can sustain unity. No particularly fine preacher can do it. Claiming allegiance to anyone other than the crucified Christ in whose name we are baptized is a source of division. And when folks over-identify with pastors this is what happens. Because no pastor can possibly please everyone, strong identification on the part of some members of the community with leaders can lead to fragmentation in the community. If you are a baptized Christian you belong to God, through belonging to Christ. If you think that you belong to the Presbyterians, or to Pastor Sarah, or to Pastor Rebecca, or to Pastor David, or to Pastor Nan, or Pastor Steve, or Pastor Kathleen… you have a problem. If I encourage you to think you belong to me, I have an even bigger problem.

My job as preacher is to make sure that you encounter week after week the God who loves us SO much that she took on flesh in Jesus Christ, breaking into this world, and through life, death, and resurrection opened the way to salvation for all of humankind. If you get caught up in my pretty voice or the way I put words together, I may well be failing you. Because it's not about me. It's about Jesus, the Jesus who bled and died on the cross, revealing just how broken we are, and just how much God is willing to do about it. That's what it's about. And when we remember that, when we allow ourselves to be deeply touched by God's choice to be known in *this* way, we get over ourselves; we humble ourselves; we can truly love others, all others, and to be of the same mind and purpose. Our petty quarrels can cease. Our love can increase. So, the report about us out there in the community will be 'Oh, how they love one another…"May it be so.

Fragile Life
1 Corinthians 1:18-25 (NRSV)

This sermon was written for and delivered to First Presbyterian Church of Lebanon, Tennessee for my final Sunday as transitional supply pastor in February of 2011.

1 Corinthians 1:18-25 (NRSV)

> *18 For the message about the cross is foolishness to those who are perishing, but to us who are being saved it is the power of God. 19 For it is written,*
>
> *"I will destroy the wisdom of the wise, and the discernment of the discerning I will thwart."*
>
> *20 Where is the one who is wise? Where is the scribe? Where is the debater of this age? Has not God made foolish the wisdom of the world? 21 For since, in the wisdom of God, the world did not know God through wisdom, God decided, through the foolishness of our proclamation, to save those who believe. 22 For Jews demand signs and Greeks desire wisdom, 23 but we proclaim Christ crucified, a stumbling block to Jews and foolishness to Gentiles, 24 but to those who are the called, both Jews and Greeks, Christ the power of God and the wisdom of God. 25 For God's foolishness is wiser than human wisdom, and God's weakness is stronger than human strength.*

***

Every time Caroline comes to church with me here, at some point in the morning she pauses by the plants in the hallway between the nursery and the church office. She has been warned more than once not to play with them, but she always stops to inquire about them. She looks at the plants and then at the floor. She sees leaves that have dropped off lying about. And asks something like "Tree broken? What happened?"

Caroline isn't well acquainted with the ways of plants. Despite semi-successful vegetable gardening efforts in her first year of life, I do not have any living plants in our house. Probably because I'm still grieving one plant. My junior year of college there was a plant sale at the beginning of the fall semester. Though I had never successfully cared for a plant, I checked it out to see if anything would brighten my room. And I fell in love with a tree-a fica tree with a braided trunk. I had to have it. I knew the perfect spot for it. I carefully listened to care instructions and then took it back to my sunny dorm room, set up the tree in the corner of the room, and followed those instructions meticulously. Every time I looked at that tree I smiled.

So, imagine my dismay when I noticed while reading on my bed one day that leaves were dropping off. At first it was just a few, but soon enough, no matter what I did, it was a constant stream of raining leaves. It appeared that my beautiful tree was weeping. And it was most certainly not a willow. It wept until it was completely bare. It was agonizing watching that tree slowly, but surely die. It was perishing before my very eyes.

Life, of any sort, is such a fragile gift. Everything dies. Have you seen the movie Wall-E? This movie opens with a view of a barren earth piled high with trash and absent of living humanity. One little trash compacting robot is busy gathering up mounds of trash and crushing them into small cubes. Though this robot, Wall-E, also gathers interesting remnants of human civilization and organizes them in his home [what is that space?] One day he finds a shoot, an actual plant beginning to erupt from the barren surface. He scoops it up and puts it into a Styrofoam cup with some dirt. When he is later joined by EVA a slick robot sent from an orbiting space ship to see if there are any signs of organic life on the planet, her mission is complete when Wall-E shows this plant to her. She, at first, and then both, spend the whole movie trying to keep that plant alive and get it back to the spaceship to complete the mission. This plant goes through far more than my fica before it first drops a leaf, but eventually it does… nonetheless, through their loving attention it survives. And this plant… it is the salvation of human life on this earth.

In our reading this morning the first verse we read was the last verse that we read last week. *"For the message about the cross is foolishness to those who are perishing, but to us who are being saved it is the power of God."* Look closely at that verse. Paul identifies two groups of people *"*those who *are perishing"* and *"*those who *are being saved."* Paul doesn't say *"*those who are damned*"* and *"*those who are saved*"* as if these were accomplished realities, he suggests that all people, different as they might be, are on the way somewhere. Perishing happens slowly over time… like a tree raining leaves. Salvation happens slowly over time… like a blossom that comes only after much painful pruning. Perishing happens. Salvation happens. These are living, dynamic realities.

And what makes the difference between these two groups of people? Are those who are being saved just better, stronger, wiser people than those who are perishing? No, not necessarily. Are those who are perishing more wicked, weak, and ignorant? No, not precisely. What makes the difference? Or perhaps I should say Who makes the difference? God. Only God. To whom we confess that we belong in life and in death. All life is a gift from God. And, in fact, our whole reading today suggests that a mark of those who are perishing, which means, by the way, tending towards eternal death rather than eternal life, is that they rely on their own gifts and capacities; they live as if they have no need of God. They boast in their own power. They live as if they are gods.

This doesn't mean that they don't talk about God and exhibit apparent piety. It means that their lives don't evidence trust in God, but rather trust in themselves. They don't witness to belonging to God. And they clearly haven't yet really met the God revealed in the cross of Jesus Christ.

Because, as Paul says, "God chose what is foolish in the world to shame the wise; God chose what is weak in the world to shame the strong; 28God chose what is low and despised in the world, things that are not, to reduce to nothing things that are, 29so that no one might boast in the presence of God." When God chose to take on fragile human flesh, and to travel with that flesh to a brutal and utterly shameful death, when God chose to make Godself known in *this* apparently foolish, apparently weak way… God ripped the carpet out from any efforts to secure ourselves with a self-righteous assurance of our own wisdom or goodness. And surely when God let Jesus walk out of a tomb three days after his brutal death, God made it clear that She alone gives and sustains life. If we meet God on the cross, then how can we be smug about our glittery glory? If we meet God at the empty tomb, why do we insist on relying on our own power? Where does it get us? Ever?

Remember, though, salvation, and perishing… they're processes, slowly unfolding, they are living realities… and as such they are fragile. Today we have the great privilege and joy of baptizing Jayne. Jayne can offer a testimony to the fragility of life, to the futility of relying solely on oneself. Today, though, by presenting herself for baptism she is offering a witness to her trust in God and God alone to save her. She is humbling herself, beginning anew, not claiming she's good enough for this, what a preposterous claim that would be in any case, but rather claiming she needs this, she wants this. And in so doing she is setting out on the slowly unfolding path of salvation, seeking to prune away that which takes life away from her and cultivate an openness to the power of God that brings her life.

And she's not making a private commitment, but rather a very public commitment. She is becoming, in a new and fuller way, a full member of Christ's church. And as I've said again and again from this pulpit, we find ourselves in church community because we need each other. And, at the same time, we are dangers to one another. We can lead one another into perishing, but we can also help one another along the way to salvation. Therefore, the practices of unity that Paul and I commended last week are so vital. And it is why the humility called for by this week's passage is crucial. Jayne begins anew her walk of faith and her life in Christ today in this community. How will you continue to reveal to her the wisdom of God made known in the cross rather than the wisdom of the world? How will you cultivate in her deepening trust in God rather than in herself or in any one person in this world? How will you help her to prune and to cultivate? And how will you help each other?

It is hard for me to walk away. But I know that it is not my power, or my gifts, or my capacities that is bringing life to this congregation… it is the power of God revealed in the cross of Jesus Christ. Don't lose sight of it. Don't let Jayne lose sight of it. Lift high the cross that all the world might see it, so that your faith might not rest on human wisdom, but on the power of God.

Hope for the Church
Ephesians 2:11-21 (NRSV)

This sermon was written for and delivered in a Summer Chapel service in Bond Chapel at Union Presbyterian Theological Seminary during my externship as a Visiting Professor of Theology in the summer of 2013.

Ephesians 2:11-21 (NRSV)

> *11 So then, remember that at one time you Gentiles by birth, called "the uncircumcision" by those who are called "the circumcision"—a physical circumcision made in the flesh by human hands—12 remember that you were at that time without Christ, being aliens from the commonwealth of Israel, and strangers to the covenants of promise, having no hope and without God in the world. 13 But now in Christ Jesus you who once were far off have been brought near by the blood of Christ. 14 For he is our peace; in his flesh he has made both groups into one and has broken down the dividing wall, that is, the hostility between us. 15 He has abolished the law with its commandments and ordinances, that he might create in himself one new humanity in place of the two, thus making peace, 16 and might reconcile both groups to God in one body through the cross, thus putting to death that hostility through it. 17 So he came and proclaimed peace to you who were far off and peace to those who were near; 18 for through him both of us have access in one Spirit to the Father. 19 So then you are no longer strangers and aliens, but you are citizens with the saints and members of the household of God, 20 built upon the foundation of the apostles and prophets, with Christ Jesus himself as the cornerstone. 21 In him the whole structure is joined together and grows into a holy temple in the Lord;*

***

I met Bob in summer Hebrew. We were both first year seminarians—he the oldest member of our incoming class; I, nearly the youngest. Perhaps you'll find it uncouth that I'd comment on age, but the way Bob would introduce himself on the first day of class, in every class we had together that year—Did Dr. Brisson have you all introduce yourselves to one another on day one of Greek School?—anyhow, we always were asked to do this and Bob would always introduce himself in exactly the same way and the way he would introduce himself gave me permission to focus on age. 'I'm Bob Hecker. I'm

64 years old. I've been a Presbyterian my whole life and a Christian these past 8 years."

Well, alright then. I'll admit it, I found this introduction off-putting-as a cradle Presbyterian who believed her Baptism as an infant was enough to bring her into the Christian fold, his declaration was... unnerving at best. But it was also funny. And sincere. And inviting. It made me want to say, 'O.K. Bob, tell me your story."

So, by the time we made it to intro theology in the second quarter of our first year, when the professors asked us to identify a learning partner who was as different from us as possible, I knew precisely who my learning partner would be. Sure, we have the same color skin. And speak the same language—sort of. And both come from the same denomination. But we were worlds apart. For 10 weeks we'd read the assigned texts on our own and write up our reflections on them and then we'd get together and compare notes. And for 10 weeks we were repeatedly astonished at the radically different dimensions we'd find in the readings. I was nervous to talk with Bob on the week we were contemplating "Who are we as human beings?" I had written two pages all about sexuality. Bob chuckled when he heard my reflections. "Hunh. I didn't write about sex at all. Shows my age!" Both of us, I believe, walked away with a more balanced reflection on human personhood than we could have arrived at alone. And, in time, a true bond of trust, love, and affection developed between us.

Bob and I have lost touch, but what I learned from cultivating a relationship with him has stayed with me—and came to me when I woke up in the middle of the night a week ago and started thinking again about this text from Ephesians. Unlike many of the letters in the New Testament, we don't know who wrote Ephesians. We also don't know precisely to whom it was written, nor why. But we have a few hints about these mysteries—and today's passage offers some significant clues. It is quite clear that the intended recipients of the letter were Gentile converts to Christianity. We heard that plainly today- Remember who you were the author says... Gentiles by birth, called 'the uncircumcision," by those called 'the circumcision"... when you were Gentiles you were without Christ, aliens from the commonwealth of Israel, and strangers to the covenants of promise, having no hope, and without God in the world. When the author tells them to remember, we learn something about who they are.

There is also a clue about who the author is, in part, it's a bit subtler, but it's there... Right from the start a contrast is established between Gentiles and Jews, two oppositional groups, calling names across a divide. The Gentiles are those who were once far off; the Jews, not strangers to the covenants of God, not aliens, counted among God's people are those who were once relatively near. Did you catch the "us" language in the passage? This, I think, is our clue to who the author was-the author speaks of the former hostility between *us*, and both of *us* having access to God through the Spirit. The you and us language throughout the passage suggests that the author was himself not a gentile convert to Christianity, but rather a Jewish Christian.

But from the very beginning of our passage it is apparent that the writer of this letter, though pointing to difference and distinction, is wanting to suggest the present insignificance of that distinction. I pulled out my Greek New Testament... I figured if many of you are doing it... well, rusty as I might be, it was worth a try... and I noticed a few things. In that first verse there is a word repeated-*sarx* - (relatively important word for New Testament interpretation-anyone? anyone?) there's an echoed phrase-*en sarki*. We can't see it in the NRSV-the gentiles were so by birth, it tells us-more literally, they were so "in the flesh"-and then the author appears to take great pains to heap up emphasis on the fleshly character of Jewish circumcision-"a *physical* circumcision made *in the flesh (en sarki)* by *human hands.*"The Gentiles and Jews were different at the level of flesh. And because of **someone else's** flesh those differences no longer need to mean division. In verse 14 we read "For he is our peace; in his flesh (*en te sarki autou*) he has made both groups into one and has broken down the dividing wall, that is, the hostility between us."

Before the coming of Christ though, as this author understands it, Gentiles and Jews were in relatively different spatial relation to the holy-far off and near-the coming of Christ relocated both groups... this passage mixes metaphors all over the place... are we all being brought closer to one another and to some place together? Or are we being transformed into one new person, made from two? Or are we being built up as a building? A growing building? Yes. Yes. Yes. Yes. Both groups, different in flesh, were without Christ before his coming—but after his coming—everything is different. The dividing wall of hostility between these groups is down... and that was accomplished by Christ overcoming the hostility between all of humanity and our creator God, by taking the whole of humanity to the cross. Through much of Christian history theologians have found in the Pauline epistles the idea of Christ as the new Adam-the recreation of humanity. Christ took all the old humanity with its divisions from one another and from God, took its hostilities towards one another and towards God, took it all to the cross—he brought all of humanity to the cross, in his flesh, as one body.

And though we don't hear an explicit word about resurrection in this passage, it's all over the passage... something changed on the cross... but surely it went into effect after the resurrection... with the breathing or sending of the Spirit onto the gathered disciples... an act which happened in Jerusalem, but quickly spread beyond the commonwealth of Israel... birthing a new community that sang songs about there being no slave or free, Jew or Greek, male and female in Christ... who preached sermons about God showing no partiality... old humanity died on the cross in one body, new humanity walked out of the tomb as one body—walked out as one body and remains one body by the Spirit.

Yes. Remains. I meant what I said. Though it certainly is hard to affirm the oneness of the Church based on appearances. How many different denominations are there? How many different versions of Presbyterianism in this country alone? (13, I think, at my last count.) And even within denominations, our congregations often, though not always, look more like one part of humanity than some representation of the diversity of humanity knit together as one. And when we continue to choose to go our separate ways when we cannot agree... in what way does our corporate life witness to the radical difference made by the life, death, and resurrection of Christ Jesus?

As much as this letter talks about this transformation and reconciliation like it's a done deal... remember that it addresses an entirely or predominately gentile community. Whether they were a predominately gentile community by virtue of geography or choice, we don't know. But this letter stresses so heavily, again and again, the unity that is gifted in Christ Jesus... so I think it was something that they needed, as much as we need, to hear... and I believe therefore that it was just as easy for first century Christians as it is for us, to segment the body of Christ according to accustomed human divisions, even if only innocuously—because we gather with those who speak our language, or live nearby—and it was just as easy then as now to believe that your fraction of the body is it—to totalize your experience of Christianity as *the* experience of Christianity. But this is very dangerous thing to do. Because Christ truly has overcome the hostility between all of humanity and God, surely, we must give up our futile resistance, and let the Spirit nudge us, nudge us to overcome all hostility, nudge us to overcome even benign neglect in the human sphere.

How does the 1st letter of John put it? If you say you love God while hating a brother or sister—what are you? Oh yeah, you're a liar. You can't love God whom you haven't seen, while hating the one you can see. We might pull back at this, start to get defensive... hate? We're good people. We're in seminary. We don't hate...but are we content to let divisions remain divisions? Are we content to call names and make assumptions about you over there as contrasted with us over here? Especially, perhaps, when we're talking about

Christians who live their faith differently than us? This might not be active hate, but is it love?

The focus for this week's worship is our hopes for the Church...we started the summer of worship in this chapel with our hopes for our time at Union... we end with our broader hopes for the Church... and here's what I hope... I hope that in the next generation of Christian ministry and Christian leadership we will do a much better job cultivating humble, loving relationships with our others—our others within the Church and outside of it. I hope that Christians, and congregations of Christians, will step out of the familiar and comfortable, trusting that Christ has torn down the walls that still seem so present—and reach out—to other Christians and congregations who look different, sound different, smell different...and even worship different-to other people outside the Church who are just plain different... especially to those whom we are most inclined to fear. I hope these acts of outreach, of peace, of embodied love—that these will start to change us—to deepen our understanding of and appreciation of our Christian faith... to strengthen our love of God... and I hope that in time our Presbyterian congregations will be a visible witness to the radical difference that Christ makes in human lives and human relationships. Because this is Gospel, good, good news that our warring and wounded world desperately needs to see... and hear.

I have a smaller, related hope, too. I hope each of you, while at Union, will practice cultivating relations across dividing lines-practice with classmates from other cultures, other political orientations, other worship preferences, other generations, other theologies... practice deeply listening, truthfully sharing, learning to love... perhaps starting at lunch today... these practices, I believe, are a part of how we are built into a dwelling place for God, joined together with those whom we would not choose to affiliate, joined together by the cornerstone of Jesus Christ.

Feel and LOVE
Ephesians 4:17-5:2 (CEB)

This sermon was written for and delivered to First Presbyterian Church of Elkhart, IN.

Ephesians 4:17-5:2 (CEB)

> *17 So I'm telling you this, and I insist on it in the Lord: you shouldn't live your life like the Gentiles anymore. They base their lives on pointless thinking, 18 and they are in the dark in their reasoning. They are disconnected from God's life because of their ignorance and their closed hearts. 19 They are people who lack all sense of right and wrong, and who have turned themselves over to doing whatever feels good and to practicing every sort of corruption along with greed.*
>
> *20 But you didn't learn that sort of thing from Christ. 21 Since you really listened to him and you were taught how the truth is in Jesus, 22 change the former way of life that was part of the person you once were, corrupted by deceitful desires. 23 Instead, renew the thinking in your mind by the Spirit 24 and clothe yourself with the new person created according to God's image in justice and true holiness.*
>
> *25 Therefore, after you have gotten rid of lying, each of you must tell the truth to your neighbor because we are parts of each other in the same body. 26 Be angry without sinning. Don't let the sun set on your anger. 27 Don't provide an opportunity for the devil. 28 Thieves should no longer steal. Instead, they should go to work, using their hands to do good so that they will have something to share with whoever is in need.*
>
> *29 Don't let any foul words come out of your mouth. Only say what is helpful when it is needed for building up the community so that it benefits those who hear what you say. 30 Don't make the Holy Spirit of God unhappy—you were sealed by him for the day of redemption. 31 Put aside all bitterness, losing your temper, anger, shouting, and slander, along with every other evil. 32 Be kind, compassionate, and forgiving to each other, in the same way God forgave you in Christ.*
>
> *5 Therefore, imitate God like dearly loved children. 2 Live your life with love, following the example of Christ, who loved us and gave himself for us. He was a sacrificial offering that smelled sweet to God.*

Words on Being

***

I want to talk a bit this morning about a recent animated film about *feelings*. Any guess what film that might be? Nope! Not *Inside Out*, though that was a contender. Definitely worth watching, in my humble opinion. No, the film I want to talk to you about is *Song of the Sea*. Perhaps a wee bit less familiar… Early in this film the young Irish boy at its center loses his mother rather mysteriously just as his sister emerged from her womb. Before she died, she told him countless Gaelic stories and painted pictures of these stories on the wall, she taught him ancient Gaelic songs as well. He was so excited meet the child in her womb. She assured him he was going be an excellent big brother. But living in a lighthouse accessible only by boat with a grieving father and a needy younger sibling, and no mother with her glorious stories and songs was not a recipe for a happy childhood. And it seems there were many messages in this boy's life that told him it wasn't o.k. to feel his feelings. His father's emotional life was numbed, and on the hardest days he took the boat to the pub. And he had a grandmother who explicitly forbade him to cry. So, it seems that the only feeling he felt was anger, all the time, and all of it was directed at his young sister—he aggressively acts out seething resentment towards this little girl who loves him fiercely. One of the Gaelic myths that his mother told him was the story of a giant who suffered a great loss and cried so many tears he created the ocean. The giant's mother, an owl witch, wanted to protect him from pain and so cast a spell to take away his feelings, and thereby turned him to stone. She then tried to protect others in the same way, turning countless fairies to stone throughout the land. There is a moment in the film when the boy meets the witch and realizes his mother's story was true, and the witch, for a moment, tempts him with the promise of no more feelings. But a strength in him allowed him to resist and ultimately, he and sister restore feeling to the witch, her son, and all the hardened fairies bringing life back in abundance.

Both *Song of the Sea* and the more familiar *Inside Out* suggest beautifully that to be alive and healthy you have got to feel *all* your feelings, even the uncomfortable or negative ones. Perhaps it's time to renew movie night. I want to share both films with you—more fully than words alone allow.

Both films came back to me as I mused on our reading for this week. One verse screamed at me— *"Be angry without sinning*. Do not let the sun set on your anger." Or as it is put in the Bibles in your pews *"Be angry, but do not sin; do not let the sun go down on your anger."* The way it is translated in both these versions it sounds like this is a command *"*Be angry!*"* It's not really a command; it's more like an assumed condition—you're going to be angry, so here's some guidance for how to live with your anger. But it was jarring, to me, to find an exhortation to anger during a whole bunch of teachings on what the new life *should* include. True confession. I don't have an easy relationship with anger. Many adults, I think, and maybe kids too, major in some emotions and minor in others—we have our comfort zones, and our discomfort zones, in the world of feeling. Given my complicated relationship with anger, I seized on the fact that later in our passage the author of the letter says to *put away* anger, along with other destructive behaviors. But I kept coming back to this earlier verse— *"Be angry without sinning. Do not let the sun set on your anger."* I think the anger to be put away, is the anger with sinning—the anger the destroys self or others, anger that tears down rather than builds up. The feeling of anger itself… cannot be completely put away.

Even people who may feel anger quite easily and naturally can get messages, especially in church, I think, that this is an inappropriate feeling. In fact, sometimes it seems to me like we somehow get the impression that *only* positive emotions are welcome in church. I've heard so many stories of the wars that can rage at home in the process of trying to get everyone ready and out the door for church and then the smiles plastered on all the faces when we walk through the doors. I've heard people tell stories of avoiding worship for over a decade because every time they step into a worship service they are transported to funerals of loved ones and they can't stop crying. And crying in church seems to them wholly inappropriate. So often within church walls someone will tell me that everything is fine, when their tight faces and raised shoulders tell a different story.

When the author to the Ephesians discusses the new life, they are to be living, transformed from their earlier gentile ways, he doesn't assume that everything will be happy, happy, joy, joy henceforth. He assumes that sometimes, in the life of faith, especially as that life is lived in human community, you are going to be angry—because you're going to get hurt. It's part of being human. Coming into relationship with Christ doesn't take that away. In fact, Jesus himself got angry… more than once. We have it on record. According to that record, Jesus didn't just get angry—he felt deep sorrow. He wept. He grieved. He was irritated. He was tired. He laughed. He felt a wide range of human emotions—I suspect he felt them all. And it even appears there were likely times when he struggled with his feelings and acted on his feelings in hurtful ways. But for the most part, Jesus seems to feel his feelings and act in love— whatever his feelings might be. He acts in ways that build up community around him, that build up individuals around him. He uses the energy of his feelings to bring positive change to the people he meets.

There are things in this world and in each of our lives that are not right, things that are not fair, things that make us angry. And there are certainly things in the life of a church that make us angry. Certain people rub us the wrong way. Changes irk the heck out of us. Sometimes it's even songs—certain hymns just hit us in the wrong spot. Sorry. Yes. Anger is a natural part of church life, as are all the human emotions. We are a human community, the body of a human, not just a divine savior. A body that feels things. But we don't only feel. We also think. And much of our scripture reading this morning suggests that we need to change the way we think in order to live with our feelings in a way that builds up rather than tearing down. And one of the foundational shifts demanded in our thinking is a refusal of dishonesty. One of the features of the old life we are to leave behind, is that it is driven by deceitful desires— I take this to mean, lies that we tell ourselves, particularly lies about the way that certain earthly pleasures will ultimately satisfy us. I get this partly from the description of lost gentiles as those who have given themselves over to doing whatever feels good. A line from a pop song came to mind—If it makes you happy, then it can't be that bad. But in fact, a lot that temporarily makes us happy leads us nowhere good—it doesn't bring joy, contentment, peace… when the momentary pleasure passes, an aching longing takes its place. But I also think that there are other lies that we tell ourselves, particularly lies about the appropriateness of feelings… lies that we must stop telling in order to truly live. Once we tell the truth to ourselves, then we can follow the admonition in our passage to "tell the truth to our neighbor" and further to do what last week's passage suggests "to speak the truth in love." Rather than pushing anger down—lying to ourselves "I'm not angry." Or "I'm not allowed to be angry." Or "I'm a bad person because I'm angry." These are all lies—rather than suppressing anger, or any feeling, grief, sadness, joy—we need to feel it, and admit we feel it, and then decide how to appropriately express this feeling—in a way that will build up rather than tearing down.

I remember a moment when an elder in my first congregation lived this process beautifully. She had had surgery, and no one visited her. She was relatively young and healthy, but she had told people this was coming—and everyone forgot. Rather than stew about this, she spoke her sadness and her anger at a session meeting—not accusing or blaming or pointing fingers. She just let her faith community know she was hurting. And she expressed that she hoped something like this would never have to happen again in her church. She may have let the sun go down on her anger for a while, but she didn't let it fester. She spoke her truth in love. And the community was helped to be stronger and healthier thanks to her willingness to feel her feeling and share it in love.

Put aside all bitterness, losing your temper, anger, shouting, and slander, along with every other evil. This is anger with sinning. Anger we cling to becomes bitterness. Losing our temper hurts people around us. Shouting brings shame. Shouting brings fear. Shouting breeds anger for anger. And slander… oh, what a terribly destructive thing to do with our anger.

But thanks be to God, we have other choices. We can't choose to never be angry, but we can choose to be angry without sinning. Be kind, compassionate, and forgiving to each other, in the same way God forgave you in Christ. We can resolve to always be kind, no matter the intensity of our anger. We can remember when we have been hurt it's often hurt people who hurt people—and we can have compassion for the one who has wounded us. By choosing kindness and compassion, we can forgive as we have been forgiven. We imitate the God of forgiving love. We can do this and more because we have been loved; we are loved; we have the love of God within us.

We are a living church. We are a church that feels, all sorts of feelings, and that loves through all that feeling. We will not unconsciously act out nor turn to stone, but we speak the truth in love, building up one another and Christ's body in this world. May it be so.

Section Five

Being Hopeful

Hope
Jeremiah 33:14-16 (NRSV)

This sermon was written for and delivered to the First Presbyterian Church of Lowville, NY on Advent 1, December 2 and 3, 2006.

Jeremiah 33:14-16 (NRSV)

> *14 The days are surely coming, says the Lord, when I will fulfill the promise I made to the house of Israel and the house of Judah. 15 In those days and at that time I will cause a righteous Branch to spring up for David; and he shall execute justice and righteousness in the land. 16 In those days Judah will be saved, and Jerusalem will live in safety. And this is the name by which it will be called: "The Lord is our righteousness."*

I am slowly making my way through a book that I know many of you have read already. It was the "North Country Reads" book last year, *A Northern Light*, by Jennifer Donnelly, a native of our very own county, I believe. This book invites us into the mind of a sharp young woman with immense potential. She is the eldest child living on a farm in the north woods, her mother has died, and she has been thrust into the responsibilities of motherhood which she is juggling along with her final year of high school. With the urging of her teacher she applies to college and is accepted but faces numerous obstacles to pursuing this dream. One paragraph in this book grabbed a hold of me and has not let me go. It is the conclusion of a chapter in which this main character, Mattie, is working in the home of her judgmental and gossipy aunt, Josie. Josie has just accused Mattie of the sin of pride. In response Mattie has the following thoughts:

> *You're wrong, Aunt Josie...It's not pride I'm feeling. It's another sin. Worse than all the other ones, which are immediate, violent, and hot. This one sits inside you quietly and eats you from the inside out like the trichina worms the pigs get. It's the Eighth Deadly Sin. The one God left out.*
>
> *Hope.*

It can feel that way, can't it? When faced with grief and pressures and losses that pile up one upon another, when reading the newspaper or watching the tv, when contemplating the poverty in this world, when hearing the sirens piercing the air only to hear later that another man has died too young in a tragic car accident, when the doctor says "There's nothing we can do", when you just can't seem to get a break, when month after month things seem to stay the same or just get worse... Hope, once a delightful gift that infused life with meaning can begin to feel like a cruel friend dangling carrots just ahead and then eating them promptly when you draw near.

It surely felt that way too many of the people of Israel at the time that Jeremiah prophesied. Their world was crumbling all around them. Jeremiah is called the prophet of weeping because most of this book is filled with dreadful oracles concerning the destruction of Jerusalem, and the fall of the Judean kingdom to the Babylonians. There were many waves to the Babylonian invasion and conquest, many waves over many years. So often it would seem like they were kept at bay, pushed back, but they'd only come back again with greater vengeance, ultimately, of course, destroying the temple and carrying off the leaders of the people into exile.

Jeremiah saw this ultimate destruction as inevitable due to the chronic unfaithfulness of the people. He uses the metaphor of the potter and his clay at one point. There comes a time when the piece that the potter is creating is not quite right and it must be smashed down for a piece to be created that is the reflection of what is intended. Other prophets though, had happier messages to deliver. When there would be momentary success in holding the Babylonians back, they would declare that Israel's fortunes were turning, instilling a "pie in the sky" hope that would only be smashed with the next invasion. This "pie in the sky" hope is rather like the hope a gambler feels when the cards go their way three times in a row, only to be crushed when the next ten take all they've got.

Can we relate to the people of Israel who were tempted to believe that what they saw was what they got? Who took the immediate circumstances of their life as signs of God's favor or condemnation, who let their hopes rise and fall like giant waves crashing against a shore? When we base our hope on earthly realities alone, we start to feel like Mattie.

Jeremiah couldn't have been popular. Jeremiah had a very different relationship to hope. This prophet who was called by God to pluck up and pull down, to destroy and overthrow, to plant and to build-in that order (see chapter one)-stuck with his message of devastation and destruction until it came to pass. By the time all this came to pass, what effect do you imagine this had on the Israelite's capacity to hope? Can you imagine that similar bitter thoughts to those that raced through Mattie's head might have taken up residence in their heads? These are the people of God; God's chosen people. And look what has come of them. Another wave of hope breaks painfully against the shore.

Our reading today is taken from a little book sandwiched during all this devastation. Scholars call it "the little book of comfort or consolation", just a few chapters that dwell on the new covenant that God is making with the people, and the hope that they can legitimately have in God. Our passage from this "little book of comfort" is not included in the oldest manuscripts we have which makes scholars think it was written a hundred years later than much of the surrounding material. A hundred years of devastation and destruction, a hundred years of waiting for a change, a hundred years of riding the waves... by then what must have been the state of the Israelite's hope? Would hope to seem cruel and deceiving?

The people had hoped, perhaps some still did, for a righteous king to lead them out of exile and to reestablish the kingdom at home. When they heard these words of a branch that would spring up out of a dead stump, a righteous branch to spring up for David, this may have led them to return to that hope, hope for a conquering king. But I believe that Jeremiah was calling them to a deeper hope, a hope for something beyond anything they could ever even begin to ask or imagine, not a reworking of something that had gone before, something radically new and different. When Jeremiah speaks of a branch shooting out of a stump, this is an image of new life shooting out of apparent death and decay, new life, newness of possibility, shooting out of the devastation, not a reworking of the devastation to make it a little more palatable or comfortable.

This could seem like "pie in the sky" hope, no different than what the feel-good prophets offered, no different than the gambler who has just hit blackjack. It could seem like cruel carrot eating hope, but it's different. It's different because it emerges from the midst of truth telling about the brokenness of the world and the lives of God's people in this world. And it is grounded not on passing, temporal realities that quicken one's pulse and make one think this time things are going to be better, but rather on lasting divine realities, it is grounded on the God who has always been faithful and who will yet be faithful.

"The days are SURELY coming," says the Lord, "When I will fulfill my promise." This is the same Lord who brought a promised child to Abraham and Sarah long after they abandoned hope that a child could come, the same Lord took a people burdened under the weight of Egyptian oppression and led them to freedom, the same Lord who fed those people with manna from heaven and quenched their thirst with water from a rock, the same Lord who had kept promises so many times before, never in expected ways though, never in predictable ways, always in radically new and different ways, but this is same Lord who kept promises before. Now this, this is a foundation for hope.

When we look back for signs that God is faithful, for stories that help us to believe in a promise keeping God, for a genuine foundation for hope, we have even more to look back on. We can look back on the remarkable step that God took to witness to God's love and faithfulness to us when God chose to be born as one of us, to take on flesh, to live among us as Jesus Christ-not as anyone expected, but better than anyone could ever ask or imagine.

The music on our radios, and the lights on our houses, and the decorations in our sanctuary suggest to us that we are entering the season of Christmas this week. But the season of Christmas is yet four weeks away. As the lighting of our first Advent candle indicated at the beginning of our service, we are now entering the season of Advent. A four-week season of waiting, preparing, expecting... Four weeks in which we can tap into hope. Not hope in the passing fancies of this world, hope in God. Not hope based on appearances, hope based on promises fulfilled and yet to be fulfilled.

In four weeks, we will sing with joy as we remember the most unexpected way in which God broke into the world in Jesus Christ the first time around. But in these four weeks prior we are invited to reflect on the faithfulness of God in the past, both as God worked in the history of Israel, but also, most especially as God worked in and through the sending of Jesus Christ, in order that hope in the faithfulness of God in the present and the future might be kindled. This does not mean that we deny the brokenness of this world and of our lives, it does not require us to deny the very real grief all around. What it does ask of us is that we do as Jeremiah did, holding the painful realities of this life in "the cradle of expectation", as one scholar put it, not abandoning the present for some "utopian dream" but affirming that whatever is present is not "the final chapter". "The world that we experience, with all of its sin and pain and misery, is not God's final word. Days are surely coming!"

Resources in addition to scripture which were cited in or significantly influenced the writing of this sermon:

Bratcher, Dennis. 2006. First Sunday of Advent: Commentary on the Text. http://www.cresourcei.org/lectionary/YearC/Cadvent1ot.html

Donnelly, Jennifer. 2003. *A Northern Light*. Orlando: Harcourt Inc.

No Ifs, Ands or Buts
Luke 24:1-12 (NRSV)

This sermon was originally written for and delivered to the First Presbyterian Church of Lowville, NY on Easter Sunday in 2007.

Luke 24:1-12 (NRSV)

> *24 But on the first day of the week, at early dawn, they came to the tomb, taking the spices that they had prepared. 2 They found the stone rolled away from the tomb, 3 but when they went in, they did not find the body. 4 While they were perplexed about this, suddenly two men in dazzling clothes stood beside them. 5 The women were terrified and bowed their faces to the ground, but the men said to them, "Why do you look for the living among the dead? He is not here but has risen. 6 Remember how he told you, while he was still in Galilee, 7 that the Son of Man must be handed over to sinners, and be crucified, and on the third day rise again." 8 Then they remembered his words, 9 and returning from the tomb, they told all this to the eleven and to all the rest. 10 Now it was Mary Magdalene, Joanna, Mary the mother of James, and the other women with them who told this to the apostles. 11 But these words seemed to them an idle tale, and they did not believe them. 12 But Peter got up and ran to the tomb; stooping and looking in, he saw the linen cloths by themselves; then he went home, amazed at what had happened.*

***

In all the times I've heard the Easter story, the story of an empty tomb, and confused or even downright terrified disciples, for years I never noticed what just might be the most important word in it; a simple, three letter word-But. It's the very first word in Luke's telling of the story and it shows up three more times in just 12 verses. The women saw Jesus' body laid in the tomb, BUT on the first day of the week they went back to the tomb. They thought they'd find Jesus' body where it had been laid BUT they did not find the body. They told the other disciples what they had seen BUT they weren't believed BUT Peter ran to check it out for himself.

This little word says "Wait, there's more..." Let's just admit up front that for the kids among us and for the kids in each of us, taking this word out of context is a cause for giggling. Kevin and I sure had a good giggle thinking up sermon titles for this one...

"God's great big but"... Go ahead and giggle. This is the joyous season of Easter after all!

BUT... let's not let our silliness distract us from the power of this three-letter word.

When I think about this word, I immediately hear a stern mother's voice saying, "No ifs, ands, or buts about it, young lady, you will clean your room." And I realize that that's a voice that lives in a lot of our heads. And it's this voice that makes it hard for us to hear, and believe, the good news of Easter. We survey this messy world, far messier than a child's room even on the worst days, and we think that that's all there is. It's a great big mess. Period. Some of us even think, convinced as we are that the story ends there, that we must clean it up, all by ourselves, "No ifs, ands, or buts about it." And this is a burdensome drag no matter how you look at it.

The women who went to the tomb early on that first day of the week thought the story was over too. They watched from a distance as Jesus bled and died on the cross. They watched his broken body being laid in a tomb. They knew the story was over. The story had ended where every human story ends, with death. They knew that death had won. They returned to the tomb not expecting any miracles, not expecting the story of their beloved teacher would continue. They returned to the tomb prepared for death. They couldn't bring Jesus back to life again, but they could sweeten his dead body by anointing it with spices. They couldn't clean up the mess completely, but they'd do what they could. They couldn't imagine that there would be a but... that the story would go on.

But it did. By God's power and grace, it did. Because of God's love, a power beyond our imagining, it did. The story did go on. The story was not finished when Jesus took his last breath. The story was not finished when Joseph of Arimathea wrapped his body in linen cloths and laid it in his new tomb. The story was not finished when someone rolled a stone across the entrance to that tomb. It sure seemed that it was, BUT there was a but... God made sure of it. God raised Jesus from the dead, allowed him to walk out of that tomb, allowed him to live forevermore. They looked for his body, BUT they did not find it. They thought he was dead, BUT he is alive.

This three-letter word has the power to change the way we see the world. Driven as we are by that "No ifs, ands, or buts..." voice in our heads, we listen to the news of murdered aid workers in Afghanistan, and more brutal violence unfolding in schools, and escalating conflict between the Ukraine and Russia, and of devastating poverty on the continent of Africa and in much of the southern hemisphere, and of countless people dying of dread diseases and we think "The world is a mess. Period." But the story of Easter, this story at the heart of our faith, begs us to put a comma and a simple three letter word at the end of that sentence, "The world is a mess, but..." I once knew a woman who told me often that she and her sister are fond of saying "God is still on the throne, and all is right with the world." That could be one way to finish the sentence considering the witness of Easter. There's also that great bumper sticker/refrigerator magnet saying "It'll be o.k. in the end. If it's not o.k., it's not the end." That could be another way to finish the sentence. There are countless, faithful ways to complete the sentence, so long as we remember that the sentence goes on only because God loves the world enough to let it go on.

If we can look at the mess of this world and see possibility and promise; if we can look even at death and see life; if we can do this... then the burden that weighs so heavily on our shoulders when we survey this messy world can be lifted, then we can realize that God is in the business of cleaning up, of making whole, of bringing life. God is in the saving business. This is what God does. And therefore, we can have hope even during the worst news. And therefore, we can find energy to be partners with God, not feeling this mess is all our responsibility, but empowered to work with God on cleaning it up, on making it right, on bringing life.

Whenever we gather for worship, we remember that we are part of the ongoing story of Jesus, a story of life that never ends. We remember that we work together to further God's purposes in this world, guiding and nurturing one another, and sharing our gifts for the good of the whole. We remember that there is a but... a great big but... for Christ is risen. He is risen indeed. Alleluia.

Let Go
John 20:1-18 (NRSV)

This very brief monologue sermon was originally written for the First Presbyterian Church of Lowville, NY, for Easter Sunday 2008; my final Easter in my first call. I delivered it memorized from the floor. I have delivered it on subsequent Easters in other calls as well.

John 20:1-18 (NRSV)

> *20 Early on the first day of the week, while it was still dark, Mary Magdalene came to the tomb and saw that the stone had been removed from the tomb. 2 So she ran and went to Simon Peter and the other disciple, the one whom Jesus loved, and said to them, "They have taken the Lord out of the tomb, and we do not know where they have laid him." 3 Then Peter and the other disciple set out and went toward the tomb. 4 The two were running together, but the other disciple outran Peter and reached the tomb first. 5 He bent down to look in and saw the linen wrappings lying there, but he did not go in. 6 Then Simon Peter came, following him, and went into the tomb. He saw the linen wrappings lying there, 7 and the cloth that had been on Jesus' head, not lying with the linen wrappings but rolled up in a place by itself. 8 Then the other disciple, who reached the tomb first, also went in, and he saw and believed; 9 for as yet they did not understand the scripture, that he must rise from the dead. 10 Then the disciples returned to their homes.*
>
> *11 But Mary stood weeping outside the tomb. As she wept, she bent over to look into the tomb; 12 and she saw two angels in white, sitting where the body of Jesus had been lying, one at the head and the other at the feet. 13 They said to her, "Woman, why are you weeping?" She said to them, "They have taken away my Lord, and I do not know where they have laid him." 14 When she had said this, she turned around and saw Jesus standing there, but she did not know that it was Jesus. 15 Jesus said to her, "Woman, why are you weeping? Whom are you looking for?" Supposing him to be the gardener, she said to him, "Sir, if you have carried him away, tell me where you have laid him, and I will take him away." 16 Jesus said to her, "Mary!" She turned and said to him in Hebrew, "Rabbouni!" (which means Teacher). 17 Jesus said to her, "Do not hold on to me, because I have not yet ascended to the Father. But go to my brothers and say to them, 'I am ascending to my Father and your Father, to my God and your*

God.'" 18 Mary Magdalene went and announced to the disciples, "I have seen the Lord"; and she told them that he had said these things to her.

***

He told me not to hold on to him, not to cling to him, not to own him, not to possess him. He told me to let him go.

There we were in the garden, standing outside his empty tomb, the man I loved and thought I had lost forever was returned to me the moment he spoke my name and turned me around. And of course, I threw my arms around him, of course I clung tightly to him, of course I did. Have you ever thought you lost someone you loved? Do you remember the first embrace upon finding him or her again? Don't you squeeze tightly, so tightly breathing is difficult? Don't you rock back and forth as your tears of sadness are transformed into tears of joy? Don't you hold them like you'll never let them go? Can you imagine then if you thought the most important person in the world to you was dead, in fact you saw him die, an awful, dreadful death, but then you heard him call your name in a garden, you saw him in the flesh, you were able to hold him again? Can you imagine?

But he told me to let him go.

And he told me to go, to go tell the others, to go share the news, the good news, to go.

He told me to go.

Wouldn't it have been easier to convince the others if I could have taken him by the hand to them? Wouldn't it have been easier even to continue to trust myself that I had not been dreaming if I were still in his embrace? Wouldn't it be easier if I could keep Jesus in the flesh with me all the time? But Jesus never did make things easy. He wanted me to share without possessing, to give without owning, to tell without holding. He wanted me to trust that the good news of his resurrection was powerful enough on its own. He wanted me to trust that he holds me even when I am not holding him. He wanted me to let go.

And so, I stand here before you today still practicing at just that. Still wishing I had my arms around him, still wanting him to be in my possession, still wishing I were in that garden, alone with him, soaking up the glory of that morn. But... I've let him go. I've given up believing that I could ever hold, own, or possess him. And I'm growing, every day, in believing that he has a hold on me. I'm here to tell you that love triumphs, that good wins, that life prevails. I'm here to tell you that Jesus lives. I'm here to tell you that something amazing happened long, long ago. You're going to want some proof, something to hold on to. You're going to want to press your hands into his wounds or wrap your arms around him. You are. Because the story sounds like nonsense doesn't it? A dead man walked out of a tomb? *"Bring him here"*, you say. *"Show him to me."*

But I invite you to let go. To release your need for proof, your need to hold, and just let yourself be held, be held in the glory of this morn, be held in the "Alleluias!", be held in the witness to the life that conquers death, be held, my friends, be held.

Nothing at All
Romans 8:38-39 (NRSV)

This sermon was written hastily on Saturday, October 22, 2005 the day after we learned that a young man who grew up in First Presbyterian Church of Lowville, NY was killed in active duty in Iraq. It was delivered in worship on Sunday, October 23, 2005 to a shocked and grieving congregation.

Romans 8:38-39 (NRSV)

> *38 For I am convinced that neither death, nor life, nor angels, nor rulers, nor things present, nor things to come, nor powers, 39 nor height, nor depth, nor anything else in all creation, will be able to separate us from the love of God in Christ Jesus our Lord.*

***

It was getting late. It was a Saturday night nearly two months ago. The wedding reception was lovely, but it was in Rome, and I had to preach, and Kevin had to play the organ the next morning, so we decided to leave before enjoying the lovely cake. We tried to find everyone to whom we needed to say our goodbyes, but one person could not be found. On our way to the car we saw her gathered with several other young adults who had participated in the wedding and we walked over to say goodbye. I approached her from behind and caught her releasing an expletive, for which she turned bright red when she turned around and saw ME, THE PASTOR. We stumbled into a casual conversation about this and that, laughing frequently, and then, out of the blue, one of these young adults asked ME, THE PASTOR, if I think the world is ending. They pointed to the hurricanes, the tsunami, the wars, the earthquake in Pakistan wasn't yet on the radar, but already enough seemed to be crumbling in the world that they were ready for a professional opinion. I was left with the feeble words of Jesus on this matter-we know not the day nor the hour... after a bizarre conversation about Noah's Ark and on to other more trivial matters, we finally said our goodbyes and I'm left wondering if I left these young adults with an affirmation of God's love and presence. I am certain that after our goodbyes they continued to wrestle internally with deep questions about the future of this planet.

I wish I had quoted Paul, instead of Jesus. "I am convinced that neither death, nor life, nor angels, nor rulers, nor things present, nor things to come, nor powers, nor height, nor depth, nor anything else in all creation will be able to separate us from the love of God in Christ Jesus our Lord."

And now this congregation and this community are in the grips of shock or are rocking with deep grief upon the violent death of a child of this church, killed while faithfully serving our country in Iraq. This shock and grief are layered on top of the layers and layers of shock and grief that have been accumulating for several years now, certainly since that beautiful September day in 2001 when four planes crashed, three into buildings, and thousands were killed. Two wars have begun and have not ended since that fateful day. Every day we hear of more deaths of young and not so young men and women serving faithfully abroad; just this year we lost the first child of this community, and now we've lost another. The shock and grief resulting from the horrors of war have been compounded by the devastation of natural disasters which seem to be occurring all too frequently and on all too grand a scale. It is easy, at times like this, especially for those who are closest to the losses, to contemplate the end of the world, for surely it feels as though the world is ending. But now, now is not the time to contemplate the end of the world, now is the time to contemplate the love of God in Christ Jesus our Lord.

"I am convinced that neither death, nor life, nor angels, nor rulers, nor things present, nor things to come, nor powers, nor height, nor depth, nor anything else in all creation will be able to separate us from the love of God in Christ Jesus our Lord."

I recently listened to a book about grief, a book called "The Year of Magical Thinking" by Joan Didion. She writes of her grief upon the sudden death of her husband of forty years, and over the extended illness of their only daughter. Before her husband died, her daughter was in the hospital, unconscious, and every night her father would whisper in her ear "I love you more than one more day." It was a message that Joan continued to whisper in her daughter's ear after her husband's sudden death. Joan also reflects on the message that she had made a practice of whispering in her daughter's ear ever since the very first day she brought her tiny baby body home from the hospital - "It's alright. I'm here. Everything's gonna be o.k." Joan struggled in her grief, realizing that she would not always be there, that she could not make good on her promises. She struggled with the one more day that her husband didn't have.

But I heard in these whispered messages of love the words of God to us. "I love you more than one more day. It's alright. I'm here. Everything's gonna be o.k." It struck me that so often we humans stand in for God, at those crucial moments when though God's presence is real and strong, we in our weakness cannot feel and know this presence. We stand in, whispering messages of presence and comfort, embodying the love of God that will never, ever, under no circumstances, that will never let us go. This struck me as I witnessed the steady stream of love pouring into the Davey household, family holding family, friends holding friends, so many tears, messages on the answering machine, baked goods in the kitchen, the loving attention paid to photographs and stories shared. This struck me as I gathered with a family as they said goodbye to a beloved grandfather this week, as we held hands and prayed, as we held each other and cried. Those of us with flesh and blood, and voices that can easily be heard, are called to stand in for God at crucial moments saying "I love you more than one more day. It's alright. I'm here. Everything's gonna be o.k." Not because we can keep these promises, but because God can and does.

"I am convinced that neither death, nor life, nor angels, nor rulers, nor things present, nor things to come, nor powers, nor height, nor depth, nor anything else in all creation will be able to separate us from the love of God in Christ Jesus our Lord."

I visited a high school friend in the hospital this week. She's on bedrest carrying twins. There's a high likelihood that at least one of the two will not survive or may survive with significant disabilities. For much of the pregnancy there has been a high likelihood that neither baby will survive. My friend Carrie has a deep faith. Lying in bed after 14 weeks of dreadful uncertainty, she quoted a magnet she once saw.

"Everything will be o.k. in the end. If it's not o.k., it's not the end."

It is this love that will not let us go that allows Carrie to cling to this profession of faith even in the face of great uncertainty. It is this love that will not let us go that allows us to surround the Davey family with our prayers and support even during our own grief and sorrow. It is this love that will not let us go that gives us the courage to hold on to each other, to whisper to each other the messages from God that we all need to hear as we confront all the layers of shock and grief that have been piling up within us.

Nothing, absolutely NOTHING, can separate us from the love of God in Christ Jesus our Lord who says to us every day "I love you more than one more day. It's alright. I'm here. Everything's gonna be o.k. Everything will be o.k. in the end. If it's not o.k., it's not the end."

In Jesus' name, Amen.

Work in addition to scripture referenced in the writing of this meditation: Joan Didion. 2005. *The Year of Magical Thinking*. New York: Knopf.

Hope in the Resurrection
1 Corinthians 15:12-34 (NRSV)

This sermon was written for and delivered to the First Presbyterian Church of Lowville on February 10 and 11, 2007.

1 Corinthians 15:12-34 (NRSV)

> *12 Now if Christ is proclaimed as raised from the dead, how can some of you say there is no resurrection of the dead? 13 If there is no resurrection of the dead, then Christ has not been raised; 14 and if Christ has not been raised, then our proclamation has been in vain and your faith has been in vain. 15 We are even found to be misrepresenting God, because we testified of God that he raised Christ—whom he did not raise if it is true that the dead are not raised. 16 For if the dead are not raised, then Christ has not been raised. 17 If Christ has not been raised, your faith is futile, and you are still in your sins. 18 Then those also who have died in Christ have perished. 19 If for this life only we have hoped in Christ, we are of all people most to be pitied.*
>
> *20 But in fact Christ has been raised from the dead, the first fruits of those who have died. 21 For since death came through a human being, the resurrection of the dead has also come through a human being; 22 for as all die in Adam, so all will be made alive in Christ. 23 But each in his own order: Christ the first fruits, then at his coming those who belong to Christ. 24 Then comes the end, when he hands over the kingdom to God the Father, after he has destroyed every ruler and every authority and power. 25 For he must reign until he has put all his enemies under his feet. 26 The last enemy to be destroyed is death. 27 For "God has put all things in subjection under his feet." But when it says, "All things are put in subjection," this does not include the one who put all things in subjection under him. 28 When all things are subjected to him, then the Son himself will also be subjected to the one who put all things in subjection under him, so that God may be all in all.*
>
> *29 Otherwise, what will those people do who receive baptism on behalf of the dead? If the dead are not raised at all, why are people baptized on their behalf?*

30 And why are we putting ourselves in danger every hour? 31 I die every day! That is as certain, brothers and sisters, as my boasting of you—a boast that I make in Christ Jesus our Lord. 32 If with merely human hopes I fought with wild animals at Ephesus, what would I have gained by it? If the dead are not raised, "Let us eat and drink, for tomorrow we die."

33 Do not be deceived: "Bad company ruins good morals."

34 Come to a sober and right mind, and sin no more; for some people have no knowledge of God. I say this to your shame.

***

I received a call one Thursday afternoon, several years ago, letting me know that Phyllis, a parishioner of mine, was nearing death. When I had stopped in to see Phyllis earlier in the week it was evident that she had declined and was not well. Her daughter, Honore, wanted me to know that the doctor had said it was likely only a matter of days then. Honore had been up to visit the day before but couldn't make it up that day because of the weather. I assured her that I would see Phyllis that afternoon and say final prayers with her. I also asked her permission to share this news with one of our deacons who had a special relationship with her mother. The permission was quickly granted.

The deacon eagerly agreed to accompany me on a late afternoon visit to offer prayers and commend her dear friend and our beloved sister in Christ to God's continuing care. Phyllis had always been a small woman, but in her last weeks, every time I saw her, she seemed smaller and smaller. It grew increasingly difficult for her to communicate, and that day she was unable to utter any comprehensible words. But it was evident that she knew we were there. We prayed, and sang, and read a Psalm. Our deacon gently rubbed her back as I rested my hand on Phyllis' hands. We stayed awhile after we were done praying and then our deacon assured Phyllis that she was dearly loved, we wished her peace, and we went on our way.

Our deacon was crying as we left the room. She had begun to cry as we sat together at bedside but didn't make that evident until we left. She apologized for her tears, but she needn't have done so. Illness and death are sad, sad things. No matter how much it may be a blessing for one to be released from earthly suffering, it is sad for those who are left behind. This sweet, sweet woman no longer looks up at visitors with a gentle smile. Even before her death she ceased to tell the wonderful stories that she used to tell. The ending of this precious, human life was indeed sad.

Often in the face of death, platitudes are offered. You all could recite them, I'm sure. Here are just a few examples. 'She's not really gone, she's just passed into another room.'' "He's in a better place now.'' 'She's smiling down on us.'' No one wants to see anyone else suffer, and it is often our impulse to try to make the suffering less by lessening the experience with our words. And often we find words that we cloak in Christian faith to try to make them even more powerful and comforting. But as many grieving people will tell you, often the platitudes we're offering don't comfort, sometimes they even alienate. They can be heard as saying "Your pain is out of proportion. It's not that bad. You shouldn't be sad.'' And if we attach to these messages the name of God or Jesus, they can become especially heavy burdens for the griever to bear. It's as if they hear, 'If you were really faithful, you wouldn't be sad.'' Is that what anyone needs to hear when they're terribly sad?

Our faith has more to offer than that. Our faith takes death very seriously. Paul suggests in his first letter to the Corinthians, the book we just completed in C cubed, that death is an enemy of God, one of many evil powers and forces that will ultimately be conquered by God. Paul paints a picture of a battle that will take place at the end of time in which all the powers of this world will be made subject to Jesus with the final victory being the ultimate conquering of death itself. There's a lot about this battle scene that Paul paints at the end of our reading today that makes us uncomfortable, but can we take comfort in the validation it offers to our experience of the tragedy of death? Our faith doesn't teach that death is not all that bad, our faith teaches that death really is that bad. It was that bad for Jesus when he hung on a cross, crying out his sense of God forsakenness and it is that bad for us, even if the one who dies is ready to die and feels closer to God in dying, those who love that person are never ready for the loss and it really is that bad. I once prayed with a man shortly before he died and his wife shared with me that he was ready to close his eyes and never open them again, but she was not ready for that to happen. This is a perfect picture of the tragic nature of death in human experience, even when the death is not especially tragic.

I am quite certain that many of you, faced with the tragedy of death likely at least one time, if not many times, in your life, through appropriation of platitudes, and the soaking up of conventional wisdom, have gained an understanding that we don't really die when we die, that there's a part of us, some of us call it the soul, that never dies, that simply passes into another room. This belief carries with it the understanding that this earthly life is something we escape; these bodies are cages that keep our souls confined.

There's something about this belief that is immensely comforting to many and has been for many years, since the earliest days of the church really. There were Corinthians who believed it, who couldn't wait to become wholly spiritual beings, to leave their bodies and this earth behind, who were lessening the tragedy of death by believing that we don't die. But this is not what our faith teaches. And when we cling to this belief, as comforting as it may seem, we cut ourselves off from the deep hope that our faith has to offer.

Our faith teaches resurrection, the resurrection of the dead, the resurrection of the body. This is a teaching that is grounded in the witness of Jesus Christ, one who died, truly died, didn't slip into another room but one whose cold and bloodied body was laid in a dark tomb, and one who was raised, not one who arose, but one who **was raised** by God from the dead, in body, mind, and spirit he was made alive, he walked out of the tomb, in the flesh, he let his disciples touch him again, he ate with them, he was alive again, never again to die.

Our faith teaches that as it was for Christ, so it will be for those who belong to Christ. We hear this in our passage today, 'But in fact Christ has been raised from the dead, the first fruits of those who have died." This language of first fruits returns later in the reading. The idea being that like the first fruits that appear at harvest time, an abundant harvest will follow. As it was for one, so it will be for many. Those who belong to Christ can count on being raised in body from the dead. This idea made the Corinthians uncomfortable. The literal translation of the phrase rendered 'resurrection of the dead" in chapter 15 of this letter is 'Raising of the corpses." The Corinthians found this idea offensive. And most of us find it creepy, or at least confusing, ourselves. I don't know about you, but when I hear 'Raising of the Corpses" I picture zombies stiffly exiting a graveyard. And when confronted with this idea of bodily resurrection, we ask all sorts of questions about how this could be, about what this means, about what kind of body we'd be raised with, about why our bodies are worth raising anyways. We'd need to keep reading in chapter 15 and need one or two more sermons to wrestle with all that.

Let me know if you're interested.

But for today, I just want you to grasp the distinction between the more common belief in the immortality of the soul and the Christian teaching of resurrection. Our more common belief in the immortality of the soul suggests something about us, that there's a part of us that never dies. But the teaching of our faith, the teaching of resurrection of the body, suggests something about God, and I quote a scholar here, resurrection suggests:

> *that God acts for those who are dead... Human beings are not immortal and do not have immortal souls; they die and are powerless unless God acts to grant life beyond death. Jesus shared this reality of human existence. He did not raise himself, or even "arise", but was raised by God. Christian hope is in the resurrection, not in immortality; it is hope in God, not in ourselves.*

This is deep hope. This is hope that validates this earthly existence we've been given, these bodies we've been given, that says that what God created, God will redeem, that says that in time, all that is broken will be made whole. Not that we will slip away to be an ethereal spirit floating with other ethereal spirits somewhere out there, but that we will take on flesh again, and they will take on flesh, and we'll be able to hold one another again, to hear hearts beating, to listen to breaths drawn. This is hope. Deep hope. And this is what our faith teaches.

As the deacon who made that last visit to Phyllis with me was drying her eyes she said *"I'm no good at this. I just don't want to let go of this world. I know I shouldn't be this way, but I am."* Nothing about our faith tells her she shouldn't be this way. God hasn't let go of the world that God created, and God doesn't expect us to either. Surely God weeps with us at all the ways this world is broken. But we know in Christ, that brokenness, that death, will not have the final word. In too many words I said to the deacon *"You're very good at this."* And then we drove home.

Resources in addition to scripture which significantly influenced or were cited in the writing of this sermon:

Boring, M. Eugene and Fred B. Craddock. 2004. *The People's New Testament Commentary.* Louisville, KY: Westminster/John Knox Press

Hays, Richard B. 1997. *First Corinthians in Interpretation: A Bible Commentary for Preaching and Teaching.* Louisville, KY: John Knox Press.

Permission granted by Phyllis' daughter and the deacon mentioned for the telling of the stories herein.

Index of Sermons by Style

Didactic/Connecting to Current Events in World and Congregation
Breathe - Genesis 13
Chesed - Ruth 4..93
Dealing with things as they are - Acts 17:16-31... 79
Feel and LOVE - Ephesians 4:17-5:2 113
Hope - Jeremiah 33:14-16...121
Hope for the Church - Ephesians 2:11-21 108
Hope in the Resurrection - 1 Corinthians 15:12-34..135
In or Out? - John 3:1-17; Genesis 12:1-4a 37
Irresistible Grace - Jonah 3:1-5, 10; Mark 1:14-20 71
It's not about me. - 1 Corinthians 1:10-18 99
MY Shepherd? - Mark 6:30-44; Psalm 23..30
No Ifs, Ands, or Buts - Luke 24:1-12 126
Of this World/Not of This World - John 18:28-40 48

Dramatic
Being Seen - Luke 7:36-8:3 (Monologue) 54
Do You Believe This? - John 11:1-45 (Monologue)..8
If... Then... - Genesis 28:10-22 (almost a guided meditation) 17
Let Go - John 20 (Monologue) 129

Biblical Storytelling
God's Giving - Exodus 16:2-15; Matthew 20:1-16 21
If... Then... - Genesis 28:10-22-..17
You Have a Name - John 20. 26

Storytelling
Company Kept - Luke 15:1-10..75
Complicated Hearts - 1 Samuel 16:1-13; Ps 51:10-14..43
Dancing Prophet - Exodus 3...65
Fragile Life - 1 Corinthians 1:18-25...104
Hope for the Church - Ephesians 2:11-21 108
Hope in the Resurrection - 1 Corinthians 15:12-34..135
It's Not About Me. - 1 Corinthians 1:10-18..99
No Ifs, Ands, or Buts - Luke 24:1-12... 126
Nothing at All - Romans 8:38-39..132

Yes!!! - Psalm 19 85
You Have a Name - John 20 26

Index of Sermons by Seasons

Advent
Hope. - Jeremiah 33:14-16 121

Ordinary Time
Breathe - Genesis 1 55
If... Then... - Genesis 28:10-22 17
Dancing Prophet - Exodus 3 65
God's Giving - Exodus 16:2-15; Matthew 20:1-16 21
Chesed - Ruth 4 93
Complicated Hearts - 1 Samuel 16:1-13; Ps 51:10-14 43
Irresistible Grace - Jonah 3:1-5, 10; Mark 1:14-20 71
MY Shepherd? - Mark 6:30-44; Psalm 23 30
Being Seen - Luke 7:36-8:3 54
Company Kept - Luke 15:1-10 75
Dealing with things as they are. - Acts 17:16-31 79
Nothing at All. - Romans 8:38-39 132
It's Not About Me. - 1 Corinthians 1:10-18 99
Fragile Life - 1 Corinthians 1:18-25 104
Hope in the Resurrection - 1 Corinthians 15:12-34 135
Hope for the Church - Ephesians 2:11-21 108
Feel and LOVE. - Ephesians 4:17-5:2 113

Lent
Yes!!! - Psalm 19 85
In or Out? - John 3:1-17; Genesis 12:1-4a 37
Of this World/Not of This World - John 18:28-40 48
Do You Believe This? - John 11:1-45 58

Easter
No Ifs, Ands, or Buts - Luke 24:1-12 126
You Have a Name. - John 20 26
Let Go - John 20 129

Beginning of Program Year
Breathe -Genesis 1 13

Index of Sermons by Churches To Whom They Were Delivered

First Presbyterian Church Lowville, NY
If... Then... - Genesis 28:10-22 17
Dancing Prophet - Exodus 3..65
God's Giving - Exodus 16:2-15; Matthew 20:1-16 21
Yes!!! - Psalm 19 85
Hope - Jeremiah 33:14-16 121
MY Shepherd? - Mark 6:30-44; Psalm 23..30
Being Seen - Luke 7:36-8:3 54
Company Kept - Luke 15:1-10...75
No Ifs, Ands, or Buts - Luke 24:1-12 121
Do You Believe This? - John 11:1-45..58
You have a name. - John 20 26
Let Go - John 20 129
Nothing at All - Romans 8:38-39...132
Hope in the Resurrection - 1 Corinthians 15:12-34......................................135

First Presbyterian Church Lebanon, TN
Irresistible Grace - Jonah 3:1-5, 10; Mark 1:14-20 71
Fragile Life - 1 Corinthians 1:18-25...104

Union Presbyterian Seminary Chapel
Hope for the Church - Ephesians 2:11-21 108

First Presbyterian Church, Elkhart, IN
It's Not About Me. - 1 Corinthians 1:10-18..99
Feel and LOVE - Ephesians 4:17-5:2 113

St. Andrew's Presbyterian Church, Portland, OR
Breathe - Genesis 1 13
Chesed - Ruth 4..93
Complicated Hearts - 1 Samuel 16:1-13; Psalm 51:10-14 43
In or Out? - John 3:1-17; Genesis 12:1-4a 37
Of This World/Not of This World - John 18:28-40 48
Dealing with Things as They Are - Acts 17:16-31 79

Index of Sermons by Topics/Themes

Being the Church
Feel and LOVE - Ephesians 4:17-5:2 113
Fragile Life - 1 Corinthians 1:18-25 104
Hope for the Church - Ephesians 2:11-21 108
It's Not About Me - 1 Corinthians 1:10-18 99

Belief
Do You Believe This? - John 11:1-45 58
In or Out? - John 3:1-17; Genesis 12:1-4a 37
Let Go - John 20 129
Nothing at All. - Romans 8:38-39 132

Belonging to God
Breathe - Genesis 1 13
Dancing Prophet - Exodus 3 65
If... Then... - Genesis 28:10-22 17
Fragile Life - 1 Corinthians 1:18-25 104
God's Giving - Exodus 16:2-15; Matthew 20:1-16 21
Hope in the Resurrection - 1 Corinthians 15:12-34 135
It's not about me - 1 Corinthians 1:10-18 99
Let Go - John 20 129
You Have a Name - John 20 26

Blessing
In or Out? - John 3:1-17; Genesis 12:1-4a 37

Forgiveness
Being Seen - Luke 7:36-8:3 54

Good News for Exiles
Breathe - Genesis 1 13
Hope - Jeremiah 33:14-16 121

Hope in Midst of Despair
Breathe - Genesis 1 13

Hope - Jeremiah 33:14-16 121
Hope in the Resurrection - 1 Corinthians 15:12-34 135
Let Go - John 20 129
MY Shepherd? - Mark 6:30-44; Psalm 23 30
No Ifs, Ands, or Buts - Luke 24:1-12 126
Nothing at All - Romans 8:38-39 132

Human Condition/Sin
Being Seen - Luke 7:36-8:3 54
Complicated Hearts - 1 Samuel 16:1-13; Ps 51:10-14 43
It's not about me - 1 Corinthians 1:10-18 99
Of this World/Not of This World - John 18:28-40 48

Human Limitations
Complicated Hearts - 1 Samuel 16:1-13; Ps 51:10-14 43
In or Out? - John 3:1-17; Genesis 12:1-4a 37

Prayer/Spiritual Life
Yes!!! - Psalm 19 85

Provision and Presence of God
Dancing Prophet - Exodus 3 65
God's Giving - Exodus 16:2-15; Matthew 20:1-16 21
If... Then... - Genesis 28:10-22 17
MY Shepherd? - Mark 6:30-44; Psalm 23 30
Nothing at All - Romans 8:38-39 132

Resurrection
Do you believe this? - John 11:1-45 58
Hope in the resurrection - 1 Corinthians 15:12-34 135
Let Go - John 20 129
No Ifs, Ands, or Buts - Luke 24:1-12 126
You Have a Name - John 20 26

Salvation
In or Out? - John 3:1-17; Genesis 12:1-4a 37

Stewardship/Tithing/Generosity
If... Then... - Genesis 28:10-22 17

Universality of God's Love
In or Out? - John 3:1-17; Genesis 12:1-4a 37
MY Shepherd? - Mark 6:30-44; Psalm 23...30
Nothing at All - Romans 8:38-39...132

Vocation/Christian life/Response to Call/Grace
Being Seen - Luke 7:36-8:3 54
Chesed - Ruth 4...93
Company Kept - Luke 15:1-10...75
Dancing Prophet - Exodus 3..65
Dealing with Things as They Are - Acts 17:16-31 79
Feel and LOVE - Ephesians 4:17-5:2 113
Fragile Life - 1 Corinthians 1:18-25...104
Irresistible Grace - Jonah 3:1-5, 10; Mark 1:14 20 71
MY Shepherd? - Mark 6:30-44; Psalm 23...30
In or Out? - John 3:1-17; Genesis 12:1-4a 37
It's Not About Me - 1 Corinthians 1:10-18.......................................99
Of this World/Not of This World - John 18:28-40 48

Women in the Bible
Being Seen - Luke 7:36-8:3 54
Do You Believe This? - John 11:1-45 58
Chesed - Ruth 4...93

www.ingramcontent.com/pod-product-compliance
Lightning Source LLC
Chambersburg PA
CBHW052146110526
44591CB00012B/1878